DETOX
your
THOUGHTS

**QUIT NEGATIVE SELF-TALK FOR GOOD AND
DISCOVER THE LIFE YOU'VE ALWAYS WANTED**

ANDREA BONIOR, PHD

CHRONICLE PRISM

Library of Congress Cataloging-in-Publication Data.

Names: Bonior, Andrea, author.
Title: Detox your thoughts : quit negative self-talk for good and discover the life you've always wanted / Andrea Bonior.
Description: 1st Edition. | San Francisco : Chronicle Prism, 2020.
Identifiers: LCCN 2019056638 | ISBN 9781452184876 (hardcover) | ISBN 9781797201443 (ebook)
Subjects: LCSH: Self-talk. | Self-help techniques. | Self-actualization (Psychology)
Classification: LCC BF697.5.S47 B66 2020 | DDC 158.1—dc23
LC record available at https://lccn.loc.gov/2019056638

Manufactured in the United States of America.

Design by Sara Schneider.
Typesetting by Happenstance Type-O-Rama.
Typeset in Mercury Text, Gotham HTF, and Zooja Pro.

10 9 8 7 6 5 4 3 2

Chronicle books and gifts are available at special quantity discounts to corporations, professional associations, literacy programs, and other organizations. For details and discount information, please contact our premiums department at corporatesales@chroniclebooks.com or at 1-800-759-0190.

CHRONICLE PRISM

Chronicle Prism is an imprint of Chronicle Books LLC,
680 Second Street, San Francisco, California 94107

www.chronicleprism.com

To Andy and our three,
worth every bit of
mental space,
and then some

And in memory
of Brian Kinlan,
forever bright

Contents

INTRODUCTION

WELCOME.

   You are here, and that says a lot. I'm so glad you picked up this book, or scrolled to this page on a screen, or are listening to these words while wondering whether you'll get a seat on the subway—I really am. And if you're wondering (or doubting) at this early moment whether this has even the slightest chance of paying off, I want you to know there is hope.

You've shown it already, by being here. There's something in you that wants to change the way you think, and at least a part of you—even if that part is the size of a walnut—is ready to do something about it.

You've most definitely come to the right place. The techniques you'll learn in this book represent the very best that research into cognitive behavioral therapy (CBT), acceptance and commitment therapy (ACT, developed by Steven C. Hayes), and mindfulness has to offer. Modern science backs up what clinical psychologists like me have been noticing for years: A lot of people have just had enough. They're anxious, stressed, and steeped in a cycle of feeling bad (and feeling bad *about* feeling bad). They have negative, worried thoughts that follow them around and get in the way of their moods, relationships, and work. Do any of these descriptions sound familiar to you?

Maybe you have tried traditional therapy or antidepressant medication, but still feel like your inner voice is your worst enemy: the ever-present itch, the darkness that you just can't get away from. You may be doing so much work to try to feel better, and yet it just doesn't feel like it's making much difference.

The numbers tell this story too. More than 20 percent of Americans meet criteria for an anxiety disorder in any given year, as that category of conditions gradually overtakes depression as the most common mental health diagnosis in the United States. Depression still remains heavily prevalent, with around 20 percent of the population suffering at some point in their lives. By most accounts, mental health problems across the board are increasing, and their growth among younger people is especially startling.

Now, it's true that more people are seeking help, which is wonderful, and therefore being counted. But that doesn't come close to explaining the whole increase. The *World Happiness Report* and the *General Social Survey* both show significant recent declines in overall happiness in the United States, even with economic upturns, which is quite unusual. People are hurting. Even those not seeking mental health help are typically reporting more stress and loneliness than in the past.

So if we know more about these problems, and have more treatments available than ever before, how could suffering, by many measures, be increasing?

We're beginning to understand the answer. And underlying it is a frustrating truth: The most common approaches to handling distressed moods often backfire. Like a crash diet that denies us the ability to feel satisfied (and as an added bonus throws our metabolism into a tailspin, making us *gain* weight—hooray!), our relationship to our negative thinking is often one of bingeing and starving.

We cajole, plead, and beg ourselves to "be positive" or to "look on the bright side." *Think happy thoughts!* we say. *Believe in yourself!* It's a very crash diet mentality—to simply banish negative thoughts and adopt a sunnier outlook. But unfortunately, the research shows that the "Just be happy!" approach rarely works. If this mind-set has failed you as well, take heart. Let's recognize right now that the typical motivational advice in this vein doesn't seem to bring many changes for *anyone*. It's not you. Not you at all.

But new research illuminates a path forward. Studies increasingly suggest that depression and anxiety disorders are not caused by negative thoughts. (In fact, every last one of us has negative thoughts at times.) Instead, depression and anxiety are caused by negative thoughts *becoming sticky*. Even medications for depression and anxiety, like SSRIs (selective serotonin reuptake inhibitors), are now thought to decrease depression and anxiety by reducing this stickiness factor, rather than just reducing negative thoughts themselves. The good news is, the cognitive-behavioral and mindfulness techniques in this book can do this too. And we've got the data to prove it.

But it does take some work, including rethinking the very nature of your mental life. In this book, I ask you to open yourself up to understanding your thoughts—and your body—in a fundamentally different way. To start recognizing in your own life the cognitive traps that zap your energy, kill your motivation, and upset your calm. You might have carried these around for years, and it will take time and true effort to change these patterns. So many of us have been sabotaging ourselves for a very long time, over and over again. And then we sabotage ourselves once more by imagining there's something wrong with us since we can't seem to get our emotional lives on track. If this is you, you are far from alone.

For more than twenty years, I've studied, taught, and practiced the science of thoughts, emotions, and behavior. I'm a licensed clinical psychologist who has long specialized in treating anxiety, depressed thinking, and the ways in which stress affects our health and relationships. I've spent nearly a decade and a half teaching about dysfunctional thinking patterns, and the disorders that arise from them, on the faculty of Georgetown University.

But many of you know me from the work I do with "everyday people." Not just my clients or students, but those who have written to me over fifteen years' time for my Baggage Check column and chat in the *Washington Post*, my blog for *Psychology Today*, or from the very first seed of this book, planted in the Detox Your Thoughts challenge I created for *Buzzfeed*.

What strikes me most is just how common the struggle against dysfunctional thinking is, across all walks of life. I've heard from so many of you over the years: a wide span across ages, genders and gender identities, races, ethnicities, education levels, sexual orientations, incomes—the problematic thinking patterns we take on are an epidemic. But as sad as it is that so many of us are suffering, we can take comfort in the fact that it connects us in a very human way. We're in it together. And whether someone is coming to me for therapy, meeting me during my university office hours with an apologetic request for personal advice, or writing a desperate note to me from halfway across the world—I see this struggle over and over again. *I see you. And I hear you too.*

In this book, I've sought to create, all in one place, an action-oriented, systematic plan for learning the techniques that are usually taught only in certain newer types of psychotherapy. So many of us know we need a better way of relating to our brains, but the "how" and even the "what" can be particularly hard to figure out. And yet, the answers are out there. They are buried in the research—but they shouldn't be. They are the light behind my clients' newfound calm; they are the Baggage Check updates I get, filled with gratitude about how the techniques have helped. Because the techniques *do* help. And now it is time for even more of you to learn these tools, to start on the path toward substantial, positive change.

So, I am here to tell you: There is not just hope. There is specific, concrete help.

And it works.

No one is a fundamentally flawed human being. Not you, not your neighbor, and not even that jerk who cut in front of you at the tollbooth. And no one's thought patterns are fundamentally flawed, either. They just need a shift, with some genuine effort and the desire to change for the better. The potential for neurological change is even baked into our biology. The type of newer, healthier thought patterns that are taught in CBT and ACT not only measurably help our moods and behavior, but they also cause fundamental, observable changes in the brain. Neuroplasticity—as much as it sounds like some sort of Botox from hell—is the quality of our brains that allows for physiological change and growth. You can change not just the way you think, but the way your brain is wired. And you can truly get those changes to stick, through practice and habit. The new pathways you build through every moment of effort with this book will become more ingrained the more you are willing to work at them.

These changes are yours for the taking. And if you are ready for this next step, there is no one "right" way to do it. Some of you will choose to read this book cover to cover, learning about each one of the tools in order, and practicing them systematically. Others will flip around until you find something that looks interesting or hits home, and go from there. Still others will quickly scan the whole book, flip to the very last line to see if it sparks a life-changing revelation, and then half-heartedly flip back through to see if at least there are any naked pictures.

(There are not.)

However you choose to use this book, though, I have two suggestions to help you maximize its effects and make the most of the precious time you spend. These are:

Read Chapter 1 no matter what. Seriously. It's not needless warm-up (we kept that here, in the intro!). And it lays the foundation of the techniques you'll want to practice throughout. This book can be consumed in random-chapter order, but think of Chapter 1 as the dough of the pizza. Without it, the subsequent chapters don't have nearly as strong a foundation, and things could very well get greasy.

And second, *make a note of what resonates with you*. For most concepts, we'll try different ways of looking at them, with different exercises, metaphors, and examples. Some will resonate, and others may make you decide it's time to go have some nachos. That's all OK. But when something clicks, keep it close. Write it down; make a list; take a picture; highlight it; keep a journal. Keep coming back to it. We're aiming for you to be able to practice and reinforce these concepts as we go along. The more specific and detailed your highlight list, the stronger and more personalized a resource you will have for yourself at the end of this process. Then we can put it all together and solidify your own individualized, strengthened plan for moving forward.

For those of you who will choose to work through these chapters systematically (and there are definite benefits to that), know that this book is divided into four parts. Each part contains common mental traps that significantly affect your mental and emotional life, grouped by theme. (Of course, virtually all of the traps affect your mind-set, emotions, and behavior, and some of them combine with each other in insidious ways to do even more damage.)

We'll begin with the traps that most affect how you think about your mind. These habits involve how you perceive your thoughts themselves, and how those thoughts fit into the larger picture of "you." Then we move to traps that affect your moment: They influence how you process the world around you and try to make sense of the here and now. Next come the traps that affect your (metaphorical) heart—habits that play into your deepest emotional experiences, and how you connect with a sense of something greater than yourself. And finally, we'll tackle the traps that influence how you think about your future and the paths you choose in life.

With each trap, you may notice that it feels easier not to try to change, not to let yourself be vulnerable. A lot of what keeps us hanging on to dysfunctional thinking is that it gives us the illusion of control, of remaining comfortable by sticking to the way things have always been. But if that comfort was really paying off for you, you probably wouldn't be here. Learning to let go of some of these negative patterns can be scary at times. But if you are willing to do it, the potential for growth is enormous.

And throughout all of this—through what resonates and what doesn't, what inspires you and what makes you remember that progress takes effort and doesn't have to be perfect—I want to remind you to be kind to yourself. Self-compassion is a very necessary part of this process. None of this is a competition to see how well you can "get" the concepts, or how quickly you can change your thinking and see results. (I see you, perfectionists!) Every step you take in reading, reflecting, practicing, and even just opening yourself up to these ideas—every one of those steps is a nudge in the right direction.

So, take a nice, full breath. Get comfy, diminish your distractions, and allow yourself to open up to change.

Let's start improving your mental and emotional life.

Please note that any personal stories in this book are heavily altered in their identifying details, to fully protect the privacy and confidentiality of those whose stories it is my honor to share. Moreover, some examples are composites of cases I have seen, or people I've heard from through my "Baggage Check" column or other media. (Except for the story about potentially peeing oneself during a CT scan. Yeah, that was me.)

PART I

Your Mind

> *"How we spend our days, of course, is how we spend our lives. What we do with this hour, and that one, is what we are doing."*
>
> **ANNIE DILLARD**

1	*2*	*3*
You Believe That Every Thought Deserves Power	You Pit Your Body Against Your Mind	You Hold On When You Need to Let Go

1

You Believe That Every Thought Deserves Power

"I THINK, THEREFORE I AM."

Sorry, René Descartes. I call bullshit.

All right, he was referring to the nature of consciousness, and he had a nuanced point that laid the foundation for centuries of philosophical thought. But these days, his words are often misinterpreted to mean "I am the product of my thoughts."

It has become a popular, so-called inspirational way to think: "If I just visualize it, I will make it happen." "You are a product of your beliefs." "If I put this photo of a Tesla Model X with premium black/white leatherette interiors on my vision board, in time it shall appear before me." Yes, your overall mind-set and attitudes do very much affect your moods and behavior. But any given thought is not truly *part* of you, and need not define you.

Actually, any given thought doesn't really say much about you at all. Some thoughts are as devoid of meaning as the ones you have while you're asleep, stuck in a dream where your old algebra teacher is a pro wrestler named Monkey Man.

Here's the thing: Far too many of us give our thoughts so much weight that they really *do* start to matter, far more than they should—and our mental health goes south. We let our thoughts gain power over us by overidentifying with them. And we pay a very steep psychological price for this.

Each and every one of your thoughts, by its very nature, has the potential to pass. But when we invite negative (or dysfunctional) thoughts to hang around, we empower them to dig themselves in and begin their long-term corrosion of the way we think about ourselves, our world, and our relationships.

A thought can't be toxic on its own. A dysfunctional thought only starts to poison us when we give it undeserved power.

It's fascinating how superstitious we can get about the supposed power of our thoughts. I knock on wood as much as the next person, but let's be real: Believing that just thinking something can make it true or that every thought (or vivid dream) has significant meaning is a slippery slope to taking power away from our real selves.

Let's try this: Visualize yourself slipping and falling into a puddle, or say out loud "I'll get the flu tomorrow." Don't want to do it? Why not? Does it feel dangerous to give "voice" to these thoughts, as though you could make those things happen just by thinking them?

If picturing a fully loaded Tesla won't make it magically appear in your driveway, then how can you summon up the flu? (Barring licking a pole on the subway, of course.)

Do we really, truly believe that just by picturing a certain thing we can make it so? Superstition turns problematic when we buy into the idea that any given thought, especially a negative one, carries this mysterious embedded power.

Reframing Your Thoughts . . . About Your Thoughts

The first steps to disempowering your dysfunctional thoughts involve what we call cognitive defusion. Defusion involves *de-fusing*, or separation: separating your thoughts from your sense of self, and also separating your thoughts from the assumption of their truth. You want to view your thoughts neither as automatically *you* nor automatically *true*.

One way to do this is to engage in what's called self-distancing: taking a step back and becoming an impartial observer of your thoughts. This helps you get out of your own head and untangle yourself from the knee-jerk experience of taking your thoughts too seriously. Some people like to do this by narrating the situation as though they were an outsider:

"Tasha is being very hard on herself right now. She keeps having the thought that she's not a good enough mother, even though that's not valid. Her kids feel loved, safe, and generally happy."

When you take a step back and view your thoughts and experiences the way you would view, for instance, a friend's, you're likely to be more objective—and less prone to unduly harsh judgments.

So let's take a moment to do this. Allow a specific concern to come to your mind: a fear or worry, something that's gnawing at you. Now narrate it as an observer. So, instead of "What I said in that email was stupid, and that's why no one responded," you would say "Stephanie is having the thought that what she said in that email was stupid, and she's imagining that's why no one responded, even though people not responding to emails is practically an epidemic these days."

You might feel hokey, but that's OK. You can even use that. ("Mike is regretting buying this book. He thinks that if he constantly has to do exercises like this, he will actually go insane after all.") It still counts as practice.

Did it make you see your present thoughts even a little differently?

To further separate your thoughts from weight they've taken on yet don't deserve, you've got to acknowledge that merely having a thought doesn't make that thought a fact. Instead of thinking *I screwed up* or *Things aren't going to get better* or *This party is going to be a disaster*, separate the thought from the assumption of reality. It's only a thought. Label it as such. "I'm having the *thought* that I screwed up." "I'm having the *thought* that things won't get better." "I'm having the *thought* that this party is going to be a disaster." For Tasha, "I'm not a good enough mother" instead becomes "I'm having the *thought* that I'm not a good enough mother," which is stripped of its assumption of truth.

So it's not the presence of our thoughts we need to change. It's how we view them. With that in mind, let's meet Maggie.

Maggie and the Worries of Work

Maggie was a thirty-nine-year-old manager at a nonprofit organization who was looking for help. She came into therapy because, in her words, she just couldn't turn off her brain—specifically, her worries about work. "I know it doesn't make sense, but when I make even the slightest mistake, I worry I'll get fired. I know there's no evidence for this, and I remind myself that I'm valuable to my organization, get decent performance reviews, and my boss recognizes my strengths, but it doesn't help. The worries start back again all the same, and they just make my perfectionism worse." Maggie struggled with not wanting to go to work each morning. Sunday nights, she'd feel a pit in her stomach, and she was beginning to worry she was sabotaging her career since her thoughts would get in the way of her focus and productivity.

She knew these negative thoughts had something to do with the pressure her parents had put on her to achieve, but knowing this didn't make the thoughts any easier to manage. "How do I get these thoughts to go away?" she asked in our very first session.

It didn't take long before she understood that if she wanted to feel better, she needed to ask an entirely different question.

Nevertheless, Negative Thoughts Persist

Maggie was trapped in the struggle of trying to "turn off" her thoughts, and she was certainly not alone. What often happens in this struggle is that the thoughts become ingrained in daily life. And they can become ingrained so severely that it feels like having a certain thought is equivalent to acting on it. This is "thought-action fusion." A particular thought (*What if I scream in church? Why am I visualizing my neighbor naked? How many germs are on my hand now that I've touched that doorknob?*) becomes so bothersome that the fear or shame associated with it feels equal to literally acting on the thought. (*I've screamed and disrupted the church service! I am trying to have sex with my neighbor! I've now made myself sick and will vomit in seconds!*) This feels terribly distressing, and can even make the person so desperate for the thoughts not to come back that they'll develop habits or compulsions in a (usually futile) attempt to keep the thoughts at bay.

Thought-action fusion is a particular problem for people with obsessive-compulsive disorder (OCD), but even those of us without OCD often become trapped in a fearful fight with our thoughts. This is because *what we resist, persists* (as credited to Carl Jung). Of course it's true that on occasion, challenging your automatic thoughts (reminding yourself, for instance, that no, you are not stupid, and that yes, your family does love you, and there is evidence for these things) can be helpful. But often, this is inadequate, or—worse yet—it can backfire. When you struggle over and over again with a certain thought, desperately begging it to go away, it exhausts your defenses. You feel hopeless and less in control of your emotions and mood, and the thought takes over even more.

Plus, when you tell yourself not to think of something, your brain starts monitoring for evidence of it. That, unfortunately, requires you to envision the thing itself—like staring at a Most Wanted poster so that you could identify the suspect later on if you were next to them at the drugstore. This mechanism is explained by ironic processing theory (which, despite its totally bogus-sounding name, is borne out by research).

Think you can force a thought out of your mind through sheer will alone? OK. Try *really, really* hard not to picture a chimpanzee in a sundress toasting you with a margarita.

I'll give you a moment.

I know, right? There she is.

A New Relationship with Your Thoughts

What would it be like to learn to live with negative thoughts, and at times even accept their presence?

Your thoughts can be important, but any given thought does not tell you much of anything about the person you are or the life you lead. Negative thoughts are sometimes just the equivalent of a party crasher or the drunken loudmouth behind you at the stadium. And anxious thoughts are often unreliable narrators.

You don't have to shrink from such thoughts, nor do you have to start shouting back. Again, negative thoughts can naturally pass through, and they can't inherently hurt you if you don't empower them. Sometimes your thoughts are inaccurate, unhelpful, or just arbitrary. But if you keep inviting them to stick, they can easily lead to decreased self-esteem, anxiety, depression, and hopelessness.

Remember: Negative thoughts stick only if they have trapped you into believing they are worth engaging with, or goaded you into an endless tug-of-war about whether or not they are true.

I'm asking you to develop a new relationship with your thoughts, which is no small thing. You learned how to think about your thoughts in the earliest days of your life, so your relationship with them is quite long-term. And you do want to keep plenty of your thoughts as your companions. You still can. But some thoughts are deserving of nothing more than you swiping them away. These are the thoughts whose profiles should scream "No thanks!" the moment you read them. If you don't engage with these bad matches, you need not be afraid of them. They will disappear on their own, because you haven't invited them over.

Eight Universal Truths about Thoughts

This new relationship with your thoughts may not come naturally at first, and it takes time and practice—but we must start somewhere. Are you ready to work on accepting the following eight truths? Make note of which are more difficult for you to believe than others.

1 The experience of having a thought—no matter what it is—is always OK.

2 Merely having a thought doesn't automatically make it true.

3 Thoughts alone are not dangerous. It is how you respond to them that matters.

4 Thoughts tend to be fleeting and pass on their own if you let them.

5 You can train yourself to observe your thoughts gently and curiously, without harsh judgment of yourself for having them.

6 Avoiding or fighting with your negative thoughts will only drain your energy.

7 The more you struggle with your thoughts, the stickier they become.

8 If you can be flexible in your thinking about your thoughts, you will develop the ability to bend your thinking, rather than letting your thoughts break you.

The Role of Mindfulness

In the Introduction, I mentioned that negative thoughts don't cause depression and anxiety disorders—it's when such thoughts become *sticky* that they can grow into depression and anxiety disorders. The way out of the stickiness involves, in large part, embracing mindfulness. Mindfulness isn't just a wellness buzzword—it literally means attending to your thoughts and bodily sensations as a gentle, nonjudgmental observer. It requires engaging with the current moment of your experience with curiosity rather than mentally checking out or running away. When you learn to let thoughts pass without resistance, you transform their very nature—and the effects they have on you.

In this sense, thoughts are like warm water. When water passes over your hands, it wets your skin, but doesn't fundamentally change its form. Your hands eventually will dry naturally, looking and feeling as they did before. But if you soak your hands in a basin of warm water for a longer period of time, the effect is different: Your skin is depleted of its oils, with an altered color and texture. Your fingers even sense things differently as they touch them. The same is true for your brain and negative thoughts. Are the thoughts passing by, or is your brain soaking in them?

Thankfully, as anybody with a hot tub habit has learned, the warm-water pruning is only temporary. But when your brain is soaking in negative thoughts, that easily becomes self-perpetuating, and the effects really *are* long-term. These toxic patterns become entrenched in your neuronal pathways, making you more likely to travel the same thought road over and over again, solidifying your tendency toward anxiety.

But back to the warm water: If your reaction is to be bothered by its fleeting presence, and not let your hands dry naturally, you'll be tempted to grab a scratchy towel and rub them raw and red. Or you'll waste your time with that annoying hand dryer, which never quite works.

Just let the water pass. It will dry in time.

Maggie, Stuck in the Struggle

Let's take a look at Maggie in the throes of her workplace anxiety. A common debilitating thought for her was self-doubt. It always showed up right before presenting something in a meeting.

> *You're going to screw up this presentation.*

She'd try and try to defend against this thought, saying, "No, I'm not. I know what I'm doing. At least I think I do. Ugh." But then the thought would see its opening and race back, leading to something like this:

> *You are. You're going to screw it up.*
> *You should have prepared more.*

And she'd feel she had to respond to the thought.

"Stop it! I can't do anything about that now. I think I'll do OK, or at least I'd better do OK. A lot is riding on this."

> *Nope, it's too late now. You're going to screw it up. Like that time people laughed at you in the assembly in seventh grade.*

"Shut up! Why do you always bring that up? I'm an adult now. I know what I'm doing."

But you still get nervous like
you did then. You know you do.
Your hands shake,
and everyone will notice.

"They will not! Or at least if it looks like they're going to, then I'll put my hands in my pockets. Wait. Do I have pockets?"

And we haven't even brought up
how your voice gets shaky!

"It does not! OK, it does. But maybe if I pay a lot of attention to that then I can keep it from happening."

You can't, and you won't.
You're not up for this. You
probably shouldn't even have this job.
But it might not be for long anyway,
because you're going to screw up this
presentation and then who knows if
they'll let you even keep your job.
You're hanging by a thread.

"STOP IT! PLEASE, JUST STOP IT! Wait, what? They're ready for me to start my presentation? Yes, Martha, I'll be right in. (Oh, shit.)"

First Steps of Mindfulness

Maggie needed a new way of relating to those thoughts, and it began with cultivating mindfulness: being curious, nonjudgmental, and gentle with herself, no matter which thoughts came up. She needed to notice and observe without entering the struggle.

Here are the basic steps of this process, which we will detail more in time:

ACKNOWLEDGE the troubling or intrusive thought, as a gentle, nonjudgmental observer. ("I'm noticing some worry about this appointment." "I'm having the thought that I'll screw up this presentation.")

LABEL the thought. ("Hello, Mr. Anxiety." "There you are, Nervous Itch!")

REMIND yourself that you have enough space for this thought, and yet it will eventually pass on its own. ("This thought isn't part of me, but I'm big enough to let it pass through me. I can watch it as it goes.")

GROUND your physical self in the moment, focusing on your breath, as you try to relax your body. ("I am here, sitting at my desk, and I am going to breathe in through my nose and out through my mouth, slowly." "Let me roll my neck to help ease the tension I always get there.")

VISUALIZE the thought passing. ("There you go, thought. You were a dark cloud, but now you're breaking up." "I'm watching that worry float by, like a leaf on a stream.")

You may now be wondering "But what about when the thoughts are true, or worth worrying about?" Right now we're focused on the negative and anxious thoughts that objectively don't deserve to retain any mental space. But in the case of those times when the thoughts can't be dismissed as invalid or dysfunctional, you need help in drawing the line between what to listen to and what to allow yourself to let go of. More on that in Chapter 3.

Maggie, Unstuck

Let's look at how Maggie put these techniques into practice. Her negative thought starts off the same:

You're going to screw up this presentation.

But it quickly takes a different turn altogether.

"So, I'm having the thought that I'll screw this up. Hi, Mr. Anxiety. I see you. You like to show up when I'm doing something important. I know you come from my history with anxiety, but I also know that I can breathe through you and you'll go away. You don't have much to teach me."

No, seriously, you're going to screw up this presentation.

"Yeah, I hear you saying that. But I'm decent at my job, and I've prepared OK. I might be a little nervous about this—most people are—but there's no reason to believe I'll screw things up, and even if I did, it would probably blow over soon."

You're going to screw up this presentation! I mean it!

"You keep saying that, but you're not in the know. You're my anxious voice, and you're typically a pretty inaccurate observer. An unreliable narrator, if I do say so myself."

YOU'LL SCREW IT UP!

"Wow, Mr. Anxiety. You're pretty wound up. Deep breathing can help you on your way. I'm going to try some nice, mindful breaths now."

Aren't you listening to me?
You'll screw it up! SCREW IT UP, I say!

"Ah, that feels better. With every inhale, my body gets calmer and I get even more ready for this presentation. With every exhale, I let you go."

LISTEN TO ME! Why aren't you listening to me?

"Because you're just not that helpful, or frankly, that interesting. And now you're getting quieter. There are far more accurate and insightful thoughts to listen to, like the way that Martha is smiling at me right now—she seems in a particularly good mood—and is ushering me inside. See ya later. I'm off to kick some Powerpoint ass!"

Creating a
New Mental Picture

Visualizing your negative thoughts passing can further help the process. What color is your anxious thought or worry? What texture? What temperature, and what size? Are the thoughts big, dark, hot clouds like smoke? Are they sharp, rough daggers with distinct edges and a piercing shine to them? Are they dirty, crumbly debris, mucking up an otherwise beautiful stream?

The more specifically you can envision your worries in material form, the better you can understand them as separate from you. This is again a part of defusion—you are de-fusing (or separating) yourself from your thoughts, no longer overidentifying with them.

Take a moment to create a mental picture of your negative thoughts, as if you had to identify them in a police lineup. Maybe guilty thoughts look different than fearful thoughts. Maybe hopeless thoughts look distinct from "I suck" thoughts. It may seem awkward to do this, but your visuals are yours alone. Plus, your brain likely already creates mental pictures as you worry, no matter how subtle—so why not steer that to your advantage? Creating a good visual also clarifies potential labels for your anxious thoughts as you watch them leave. (Goodbye, "Worry Shard" or "Nervousness Blob"!)

Now, envision what the disappearance of those thoughts could look like. Not through beating them to a pulp, but by their gradually losing strength as you disengage from them. A clear visual further helps you to separate yourself from the thoughts and let them pass. Here are a few examples that my clients have used.

How Do You See Your Negative Thoughts?

Negative Thought	How It Passes
Cold, hard ice	Gradually melts and disappears entirely
Thick, dark smoke	Eventually dissipates and moves past to reveal a blue sky
Crunchy, black dirt	Flows down the drain as you wash your hands
Leaves on a stream	Float down a waterfall and steadily pass as the stream continues flowing along
Loud, active birds	Gradually disappear, getting quieter as they fly away
Words floating away	Slowly and peacefully rise up out of sight

Thought Metaphors

Sometimes, the thoughts feel too big—or too plentiful—to fit into a single visual. Maybe you have too many anxious thoughts at once, and they don't even feel related to each other. Or one thought feels too overwhelming to be contained in concrete form. Or maybe you just have trouble visualizing things in general. (It's estimated that 2 to 5 percent of people lack a "mind's eye"—a condition called "aphantasia"—and truly can't call an image to mind voluntarily. It has only recently begun to be studied.)

If any of these apply to you, you may be more of a conceptual metaphor person. Try on one of these ACT (acceptance and commitment therapy) analogies for size the next time your worried thoughts threaten to stick.

A THOUGHT PARADE: You are sitting in a comfy chair on the parade route, watching your thoughts go past. Some parade floats/thoughts are enjoyable (*I think there's still ice cream in the freezer!*), whereas others are loud or obnoxious, tossing some cheap plastic giveaway right at your face (*You'll never amount to anything!*). But every float/thought passes on its own as you sit; you need not do anything.

A PASSING STORM: You are sitting in a sunroom, looking out at a darkened sky. You hear the crackle of thunder, marking the beginning of a storm (your latest round of worries), but as you continue to sit, you notice that the clouds eventually pass by, revealing a clearer sky and bright sun as they disappear.

PASSENGERS ON A BUS: You're driving a bus. Passengers (your thoughts) get on, and passengers get off. Some stay longer than others, but they all eventually leave the bus. Some smell; some yell; some even tell you you're taking a wrong turn. And some smile and make your day. Either way, you know your route and it's not up to you to do anything but keep driving the bus.

When the Visual Is the Problem

Perhaps the mental intrusions you're trying to let pass are actual visuals themselves. You keep seeing yourself screwing up on that date, for example. Or you see the face of someone you have hurt. Or you visualize your newly licensed daughter getting into a car crash every time she takes the keys. (If your image is one that is especially horrifying and induces feelings of panic too intense to manage on your own, please don't push yourself. You may consider getting individual help for your trauma, in addition to using some of the tools in Chapter 2 about your bodily reactions, and in Chapter 3 about letting go.)

You can defuse from a visual as well, and the same principle applies: Acknowledge it and allow it to go, watching it pass. Remember, you need not run from the image. The goal is to recognize it for what it is: Something that will pass on its own.

Here's one technique: Take the troubling image and visualize it as a photo file on a computer. Now, play around with it. As anxiety-provoking as the image may be, it is only a photo, the same way the visual in your mind is just an image. Stretch it. Rotate it. Make it black and white. Use different filters. Add a caption ("The Tale of Carlos's Terrible Incompetence on Dates" or "The Blockbuster Horror Film of Mom's Greatest Fears"). If it's the equivalent of a mental video, speed it up. Play it in herky-jerky slow motion. Add a "Subscribe to my channel for maximum anxiety!" button. Chop it up into various cuts out of order. Play it backward.

The purpose of this is to remind yourself that a mental visual need not be any more true, meaningful, or powerful than a photo file on your laptop. Observe it, but don't buy into its value. You can neutralize it this way—disempowering its ability to stick and bother you.

Approaching Things Differently: Hearing Your Thoughts

Continued practice helps the defusion process come much more naturally. You might need to spend at least a full couple of minutes with the techniques, several times over different days in different contexts, to help them click.

But if metaphors and visuals aren't helping you distance yourself from your thoughts, what about hearing them differently?

MAKE THE THOUGHT MUSICAL. Put the words of the thought into a song. Anxious rumination over having put your foot in your mouth at a social event certainly seems less dire when it becomes "Well, I messssssssssed up today, day, day, day, day-ay" to the tune of "Shake It Off." Or maybe you prefer "I may have a di-sease, ease, eeeeeeeeease"—to the tune of "I Want to Hold Your Hand."

TRANSLATE THE THOUGHT INTO A DIFFERENT LANGUAGE. The more foreign to you, the better. Say it several times in this new language, or choose one that sounds the strangest (fun with online translators!). *Kumppanini vanhemmat vihaavat minua* doesn't quite have the same impact in Finnish as it does in English ("My partner's parents hate me"), does it? Does this help you remember that ultimately, the thought is just words?

SAY THE THOUGHT IN A SILLY VOICE. Maybe it's a snooty, hoity-toity, high society accent declaring, "Your child got in trouble at school, and now they're in for a lifetime of crime. They shall be in jail by adolescence."

PRACTICE:

Viewing your thoughts
as an observer

Work on thinking of your negative thoughts as fleeting occurrences that you are big enough to make room for, but that will pass naturally on their own.

1 **COMMIT** to acknowledging that your thoughts are occurrences that pass, separate from your essential essence, and they never define you. Return to the Eight Universal Truths about Thoughts (page 21) and start putting them into practice.

2 **IDENTIFY** your most distressing negative thoughts in the moment, and practice acknowledging the thoughts, labeling them, and watching them pass.

3 **CREATE** a visualization to help this process along, giving concrete form to your thoughts as you picture them like objects that are separate from you. Breathe slowly and deeply while picturing your thoughts passing on their own. Add a metaphor, a distinctive voice, or a song that strips them of their power.

2

You Pit Your Body Against Your Mind

IF I WERE TO COME at your toe with a hammer, right here, right now, then not only would you probably stop reading the rest of this book and instead focus on taking legal action, but you would also experience some toe pain. Where is that pain felt? In your toe?

Nope. It's in your brain.

There really is no line between a mental experience and a physical one, since it's your brain that processes sensory experiences—from pain to pleasure, hot to cold, muscle tension to the buzz of a tequila shot. In fact, there is even similar neurotransmitter activity between the experience of social rejection and that of physical pain. Grief and loss often result in true and tangible chest pain—no doubt the origin of the "broken heart." A "pain in the neck" is often felt quite literally as well.

Your brain *is* your body. The brain—though responsible for processing the most profound and indescribable human experiences, and performing cognitive calculations that defy the most complex supercomputers—is a physical organ, as real in the material sense as your heart or your lungs.

So how do you feel emotions, physically? A lot of my clients are surprised to discover how many ways their moods are reflected within their bodies, once they really start paying attention. Here are some common physical manifestations of emotions.

ANGER: Tight jaw, hot chest, clenched fists, shallow breathing, increased heart rate, pounding head, the urge to yell

ANXIETY OR FEAR: Butterflies in your stomach, clamminess, irregular heart rate, tingling in your limbs, dizziness, shallow or difficult breathing, tension in your neck and other muscles, the urge to flee

SADNESS: Hollow chest, sunken facial muscles, sluggishness, chest pain, a sensation of a weight on you, the urge to cry or curl up in ball

GUILT: Weight in the pit of your stomach, inability to relax

SHAME: Nausea, prickly feeling in the face, the urge to cover your head and avoid others

Do you recognize yourself in any of these sensations? Are there other feelings you have that aren't listed here?

What Is "Frustration"?

Another emotion you might recognize in your body is frustration. Frustration is a descriptor a lot of us use even more frequently than anger, sadness, or fear. It may even feel like a regular part of life for you: frustration with a boss who sets unclear or impossible expectations, or with a partner who doesn't carry their weight within the relationship. While being frustrated most definitely tells us we're experiencing an elevated stress response, frustration itself is often not the original emotion—it's a reaction to it, a layer on top of it. For instance, frustration can come from:

ANGER: Like when your teenager knows their curfew, but repeatedly refuses to follow it

ANXIETY OR FEAR: Like when your partner is in the ER waiting room for the second straight hour, and still unable to see a doctor

SADNESS: Like when you've tried to reach a goal unsuccessfully over and over, and now feel helpless and hopeless at your inability

GUILT: Like when a friend is sullen to you after you said something hurtful

SHAME: Like when a coworker repeatedly brings up a mistake you made in the past

Frustration could describe any of these situations. And that feeling is most certainly real. But the emotion beneath it is very different in each example. Frustration can be seen as the distress that stems from things not going as we want them to. It involves feeling blocked and lacking a sense of control and predictability over a situation (which significantly increases the body's stress response). But to gain clarity on how to unblock yourself, you must address the additional emotions beneath the frustration. The next time you feel the familiar twinge of frustration, dig deeper. What additional emotion needs to be understood?

Start by Observing

It's time to start observing physical sensations as we observe our thoughts—in the same gentle, nonjudgmental way, of course. Now, there may be nothing gentle about a pounding heart or a throbbing head. But just as our thoughts don't define us, neither do our physical sensations.

Observing our physical sensations gently won't make them disappear. Chronic pain, for instance, can be unrelenting, and the struggle with it can affect the totality of someone's daily experience: moods, attitudes, actions, and interactions. But the interplay between mind and body should not be ignored, with intriguing new research suggesting that depressive episodes and traumatic experiences even change the way that pain receptors work, putting people who suffer from those experiences at higher risk for chronic pain.

We must also recognize how easy it is to get stuck in a self-perpetuating trap. The mind-body interplay goes both ways: Bodily sensations affect our thoughts, and thoughts can in turn cause bodily sensations. The sensations make the thoughts worse (*It is so hard to walk up these stairs; ugh, I am going to be late again and will probably get fired!*). And the thoughts in turn make the physical sensations harder to bear (*If I get fired, could I even get another job? Can my body even handle that? I am so weak—why do my legs feel like this? They feel even worse than a moment ago!*). If you have ever run in a race, you may have been caught in the throes of this cycle: The weaker and more exhausted you felt physically, the more your self-doubt crept in, which highlighted further how miserable your body felt. The good news is, we can untangle ourselves with attention to this cycle.

How you interpret your physical sensations matters more than the sensations alone. And just as the same thought can be interpreted very differently by an anxious versus a non-anxious person, so too can the same physical sensation.

The arousal of the peripheral nervous system, for example, can be interpreted as excitement—or as terror. Let's talk roller coasters. Do you enjoy them? Is the pounding heart, shortness of breath, and sinking feeling in your stomach at the top of a ferocious coaster's signature drop something that you adore? Or does it make you think you're going to die, and you'd rather have nineteen back-to-back colonoscopies than ever experience it again?

The objective physiological sensations experienced by a roller coaster aficionado and a roller coaster hater aren't that different. It's how you make sense of the sensations—how you interpret them, what lens you see them through, what story you tell yourself about them—that differs. For the roller coaster fan, these sensations are welcome, and they're interpreted in a positive way. So they feel good. For the coaster-hater, they are unwelcome and feared, and feel terrible.

Both judgments are valid, of course. But for many of us, that roller coaster is our normal daily life. We are not at the top of a hill on a ride called The Cannibal, but instead just on a work conference call, going to the doctor, speaking up in class, or talking to someone at a bar. And as our nervous system arousal increases, we may interpret it in a helpless, negative way.

To keep from feeling out of control at these times, you must look at your physical sensations in a different way, to let them work for you, rather than against you.

Reinterpreting Our Physical Sensations

A while back, I had to have a CT scan of my kidneys, with dye. Before the technician injected the dye, she said something surprising: "Oh, just so you know—when the dye starts coursing through, a lot of people have the sensation that they're about to pee themselves. It may even feel like you *are* peeing. It's nothing to worry about. You aren't peeing."

Granted, this was just the seventh-most fun part of the whole CT scan experience, but I was grateful for the reassurance. I thought it was funny and beside the point—until the sensation actually began in my own body. I had never felt something with such physical certainty in my life: I was sure I was peeing, right then, right there, in the scanning machine. (*Holy shit!*) The sensation was as real as my heartbeat or the sound of the machine. But I took a breath and chose to trust what the technician had told me. I was not *truly* urinating on myself. That physical sensation—though totally real—was highly prone to misinterpretation, and I needed to adjust my assessment of it. I could observe the sensation, but I needed to realize that the sensation was an unreliable narrator. That sensation was—please forgive me for this—fake news.

Once I made this mental adjustment, the sensation no longer brought any of the anxious thoughts or dread that it had before. Had the technician not warned me, I would have continued to be certain that I was incontinent there in the middle of a CT scan, and that would have been quite distressing. Instead, I was free from anxiety about it. Why? *Because I trusted my reinterpretation of the sensation.* I knew that reality was different than what the sensation was trying to make me think.

Believe me: If I can convince myself that I'm not really peeing, even though every nerve in my body, equipped with thousands of years of evolutionary insight, is telling me that I am, then virtually any bodily sensation is reinterpretable. Almost any physical feeling can be adjusted to have a less catastrophic mental effect. This becomes especially crucial given how anxious thoughts increase anxious physical sensations—the dreadful cycle that people who suffer from panic attacks know so viscerally. Yet anyone who has had treatment for panic knows that the hitch in your heartbeat, slight sensation of your throat closing up, or subtle sense of lightheadedness are just that. Individual sensations. They are not synonymous with a full-fledged attack, and they need not turn into one. They cannot conspire against you if you do not empower them.

So that is our goal for you as well: to reinterpret uncomfortable sensations in a less catastrophic way. Practice acknowledging that individual anxiety symptoms cannot hurt you on their own. If your brain processes them nonjudgmentally and interprets them in a neutral way, they won't progress to Vicious Cycle Land.

Tony and Feeling "Off"

Twenty-eight-year-old Tony came to me in frustration after his doctor told him that all his tests said he was "fine." He had felt, in his words, pretty awful physically and mentally for quite a while, and it seemed to date back four months to when his apartment was broken into while he was vacationing. He frequently felt "off," which sent him into a tailspin of skipping consecutive days of work and isolating himself at home instead of seeing his friends. He had headaches, nausea, and chest pain. He often felt dizzy and had trouble sleeping.

Tony was willing to believe that the break-in had something to do with his symptoms, and indeed was relieved that his medical tests had ruled out various physical ailments, but he couldn't understand why something that he didn't even witness could cause such a traumatic reaction. He also felt helpless to do anything about his symptoms, no matter what was causing them. Most of all, Tony felt scared that these feelings would never go away, which debilitated him further. He felt hopeless and helpless, and at first glance could easily be described as depressed. Fortunately, there was plenty of help and hope to offer Tony, and it began with learning about the ways the body is designed to react to threat.

Fight, Flight, or Freeze

Tens of thousands of years ago, our bodies developed ways of handling threatening situations (best practices for a life-or-death showdown with a saber-toothed tiger). These physiological responses were solidified and passed down through years of evolution. Here's what happens to your body in fight, flight, or freeze mode:

1. Your brain perceives a threat.
2. It sends signals to your body to mobilize its physical defenses.
3. You now have the added strength and agility to fight the threat or flee from it. (Some people will freeze.)

In modern life, the drawbacks of the "mobilize physical defenses" part of fight-or-flight are often more significant than the benefits. Let's look at them individually. You'll notice how the very same action within your body—intended to be a benefit—can instead become a serious problem.

Changing the Narrative

In modern life, the threats we face tend to be more subtle—they are social and emotional. They are chronic worries rather than immediate dangers. So the fight-or-flight response formulated to save our lives turns out to be more likely to screw with our brains.

It can even screw with us physically. When your hypothalamic-pituitary-adrenocortical (HPA) axis—which, if your body's stress response was a city, could be considered the plumbing system—secretes the stress hormone cortisol into your bloodstream over and over again, your body and brain get worn down. They stop resetting back to their baseline normal modes over time, and you start walking around in a chronic stress response.

Your Body's Response

Process	Benefit	Drawback	Anxious Voice
Heart Rate	Increases, to boost blood flow to muscle groups.	Your heart feels like it is going to beat out of your chest, like you are having a heart attack.	*Can others hear that? What is wrong with me?*
Circulation	Blood flows away from your fingers and toes and toward bigger muscles, energizing them to keep you safe.	Your fingers and toes feel numb, cold, shaky, and tingly.	*I can't seem to even hold on to these papers! Everyone can see me shaking!*
Breathing	Gets shallower, to preserve oxygen for major muscle groups so the muscles can react better.	You start to hyperventilate and feel like you can't get enough air.	*I can't breathe! Am I having a heart attack?*
Digestion	Stops, to allow the body to concentrate its resources on more immediate concerns.	Your lunch is sitting in a sea of stomach acid, making you feel sick.	*Oh my God, now I might throw up!*

Process	Benefit	Drawback	Anxious Voice
Vision	Pupils dilate, increasing your ability to take in the entire scene and maximize threat detection.	Your vision feels fuzzier, light becomes glaring, and you may even have some black spots in your visual field.	*I can't see straight! What is happening to me?*
Skin	Your hair stands on end, making you appear bigger to predators.	You get the feeling of chills or goosebumps.	*This is so unnerving!*
Perspiration	You start to sweat, since your body generates heat through increased energy.	You feel cold and clammy, to say nothing of your embarrassing armpit stains.	*Now I can't even lift my arms or everyone will see!*
Muscle Tension	Your muscles are activated for action, so they can summon all their strength to run, fight back, or ward off an attack.	You're so tense you can't relax or feel comfortable.	*I'm a ball of nerves right now, and my neck hurts!*

The stress response can feel out of your control, but you have far more power than you realize.

When you break the thought-sensation cycle, you neutralize the effects of fight or flight. By reinterpreting fight-or-flight sensations as your body just doing its job—remembering the benefits rather than getting carried away in the flood of drawbacks—you protect yourself immediately.

You become hypervigilant and hypersensitive to any negativity whatsoever ("What are *you* looking at?"). And these changes tend to stick, because your brain has less energy and strength to rewire itself and create new pathways. To top it all off, your hippocampus—typically dependable for shutting off the stress response and letting you relax again—begins to feel the wear and tear of long-term stress, and doesn't work as well anymore either.

The damage is real, though it's not irreversible.

Changing the narrative involves, you guessed it, observing your thoughts gently and nonjudgmentally, even as your symptoms pick up. Can you catch the thoughts about your sensations that are unreliable and unhelpful, and let them go? And can you reframe the situation in a more realistic, functional, accepting way? Here are some examples:

LET PASS	EMBRACE
I can't handle this.	I have the tools to get through this. A calmer mind can help calm my body.
My body is out of control.	This feels hard to get through, but it is a natural response and my body is built to handle it.
This is terrifying.	This feels scary, and that's OK. I am safe and have the ability to get through this.
What is happening to me?	This is a natural stress response, and when I work to calm my body down, it will begin to go away.

LET PASS	EMBRACE
What if this never goes away?	It feels intense now, but this is a response that always passes with time.
What is wrong with me?	Anxiety naturally feels bad sometimes. But I am learning to breathe through it and tolerate it.

Stopping the Mood Killers

Your body's role in your moods doesn't just come and go. To get real about making positive changes, you must take an honest look at the big picture of your overall day-to-day habits.

Good health habits aren't about worshipping at the altar of kale. Balance is key, not only to keep from denying yourself a treat every now and then, but to keep from overdosing on supposedly "good" stuff as well. Too much spinach can give you kidney stones (hence my infamous CT scan). Too much sunlight can burn you. Too much exercise can weaken you. The list goes on.

The physical habits below have crucial effects on your everyday mood. Are you willing to examine your behaviors nonjudgmentally, but realistically? At this stage, the goal is awareness. In Part IV, we'll talk about tools to put better habits in place.

MOVEMENT: Regular physical exercise has significant antidepressant and anti-anxiety qualities. You don't have to join a gym to experience its benefits. Even a consistent commitment to walking brings mental and physical boosts.

SLEEP: Evolution dictates that lack of sleep can lead to higher levels of anxiety. (It's your brain's way of overcompensating for your sluggishness: If you err on the side of viewing everything as a threat, then you're less likely to be eaten.) On average, American adults get less sleep now than they did a generation ago, and there's considerable evidence it's less restful sleep, too, in part because of the stimulation of our phones. Just committing to a bedtime that is fifteen minutes earlier, or not taking your phone into your bedroom, can help improve sleep.

HYDRATION: Dehydration causes mental fogginess and fatigue, both of which contribute to a plummeting mood. In extreme forms, this can even mimic the effects of a panic attack. With a large percentage of your body—including your brain—made up of water, it's imperative to keep up a steady intake to counteract what is lost through sweat and urine. Choose a reusable water bottle that you enjoy having around and like looking at, and make a commitment to working your way through it at least twice per day as a start.

CAFFEINE: Excessive intake of caffeine—understandable in our increasingly sleep-deprived society—packs a double whammy. Not only do caffeine's stimulant effects in high doses make you more jittery and anxious, but dependence on caffeine can make you feel sluggish and out of sorts when you don't get enough. To cut down, start slowly, by increasingly mixing in some decaf, substituting a cup of herbal tea, or diminishing the size of your coffee mug.

SUNLIGHT AND NATURE: Open, green spaces have a calming effect on our senses. This is another evolutionary adaptation, since the ability to see the horizon assured us that no predators were creeping up, which allowed us to relax. Daylight helps regulate mood, which is why people who suffer from seasonal depression can be helped by light boxes that replicate the wavelength of sunlight. Bringing nature inside, as with houseplants, can soothe peripheral nervous system agitation as well.

LACK OF NOVELTY: Behavioral ruts can lead to mood ruts and a sense of stagnation. While all of us have different thresholds for how much adventure we want in our lives, we each need at least a bit of novelty to keep us stimulated, motivated, and engaged. From trying a new cuisine to painting your entire home, your brain gets a boost when you expand beyond your same old, same old.

NICOTINE: As a stimulant, nicotine traps many people in a cycle of dependence as their number-one lifeline in times of stress. And when they have to go without it, moods take a dive. To begin cutting down, focus not just on the number of times you smoke or vape, but on substituting an alternative stress reliever when you're most desperate for the hit. More on that in Part IV.

ALCOHOL: Alcohol use can easily grow problematic without your noticing, especially because it briefly takes the edge off anxiety. Does a drink bring you relief to the point where you always choose it first, before considering other options that will be more long-lasting? Are there times when your drinking does more harm than good?

MARIJUANA: The research is as varied as the people who use it: For some, marijuana is a tool in the fight against chronic pain, or just an occasional relaxant. For others, it becomes not a help but a hindrance, masking underlying depression or anxiety that keeps getting worse while you convince yourself more and more that you need marijuana to get through the day. Ask yourself what role it has for you: Does it enhance, or does it block you from moving forward or dealing with something you need to?

OTHER RECREATIONAL DRUGS: From opioids to stimulants to hallucinogens, we could spend chapters more on the variety of drugs that Americans consume, whether prescription or non-, whether microdosing or bingeing. Recreational opioid use tends to be the most risky, as the cycle of tolerance and dependence can lead to addiction quite quickly—even if the pills were painkillers originally prescribed legitimately by a doctor. Look for patterns in what you rely on to get through your day or week. Has your use increased over time? Is your tolerance increasing? What about cravings, or potential withdrawal symptoms? Does the drug take up more space in your life—financially, emotionally, or logistically—than you are willing to acknowledge?

SCREEN TIME: Many of us spend more hours on screens than we do sleeping. Do you have a sense of where and how your devices fit into your daily life? A healthy balance can be hard to come by, given how self-reinforcing various apps and online behaviors can be. We'll talk more about these habits in Chapter 7, but they most definitely deserve attention when you're looking at the big picture.

FOOD: Food should generally work for you, not against you—sustaining you and making you feel satisfied and strong. The trap is in the extremes, whether through over-restricting yourself or bingeing to escape uncomfortable feelings. Is your diet varied enough that it allows your brain to function well and keeps your vitamin and mineral levels in their proper ranges? There is a growing body of research that points to the oft-cited Mediterranean diet—full of vegetables, fruits, lean proteins, and omega-3 fatty acids—as being beneficial in fighting depression.

HORMONES AND THYROID FUNCTION: Though controversy exists about exact optimal ranges and when intervention is called for, hormones' effects on mood and anxiety are well documented. Low thyroid function can bring you down mentally and physically, whereas hyperthyroidism may bring on symptoms of anxiety. When's the last time you had a full medical checkup, with blood work?

MEDICATION: It's important to be fully versed in how your medications interact with each other, and how they mix (or not) with alcohol, caffeine, and your diet. Even a medication that works wonders can become a nightmare if it is taken incorrectly or combined in a problematic way with something else. Commit to reading—I mean fully reading—the warnings and considerations on your prescriptions and supplements. And if there is anything of concern, take the time to reach out to your doctor or pharmacist.

SEX: For many people, the physical release of regular sexual experiences is an important part of feeling balanced, especially when it's combined with emotional satisfaction. Orgasms—whether alone or with others—can have measurable anxiety-reducing effects. Yet sex has the potential to feel uncomfortable or distressing if it is not fully autonomous.

Being honest with yourself about the effects of your sexual life—or lack thereof—can illuminate connections with your overall mental well-being.

Tony's Vicious Cycle

Tony—who had been feeling physically miserable ever since his home was broken into—and I had a lot to figure out. And when we dug deeper into his physical symptoms, their triggers, and their effects, it became clear that it wasn't the actual physical symptoms that were most debilitating. It was his fear and frustration *about* his symptoms: the way he viewed them, and in turn how that interpretation made him feel (and behave). When Tony spent a week observing and labeling his thoughts when he felt at his worst, a striking pattern emerged: Instead of being functional or helpful, these thoughts all contributed to his sense of fear, hopelessness, and lack of control. That in turn heightened Tony's physical anxiety, which made the symptoms even stronger.

Common among Tony's thoughts were:

This has happened for months now. I'll never feel normal again.

My friends probably think that I'm lame, or faking, or flaking out.

I bet my body is damaged and doesn't remember how to feel good.

How will I ever go to that conference if I feel like this?

That doctor probably screwed up my tests.

I bet therapy won't help, and then what?

I'm never going to get a good night's sleep again.

When Tony would get most upset in our early sessions, it wasn't because of the physical discomfort. It was instead because he was ruminating on the *implications* of his discomfort—and how they meant that something scary and bad was wrong with him that he couldn't control. His sleep was also disrupted far more than he had realized. When I had him track it, he discovered that he was lying in bed listening for unusual sounds for at least an hour or two each night, and waking up far more than normal. This perpetuated his feelings of exhaustion.

Adjusting the Lens

Tony and I did a crash course on all the ways his body was signaling to him that it was still on high alert, four months after the break-in. The headaches (which got worse when his neck and shoulder muscles tensed), dizziness, chest pain, and nausea were signs that his peripheral nervous system was in overdrive. But this didn't mean that something was wrong with him. Instead, we reframed this as his body trying to cope, doing what it was built to do through years and years of evolution.

Tony had been affected greatly by the break-in, and that made sense. It was a violation on the most visceral level: His space, his sense of security, and his treasured possessions were all threatened and intruded upon. His body was designed to react to that threat, not ignore it: to pay heightened attention to strange noises, and to keep him awake and hypervigilant to his surroundings. His muscles were pumped, his heart ready to race to help him pounce on an intruder. Tony's body was doing what it was supposed to, *if it were still under siege.*

So our work was to stop pathologizing these bodily reactions and viewing them as the enemy. Instead, Tony began to identify them as an understandable, natural physical response—which neutralized the threat they represented. Tony also needed to let his body learn that it was no longer under threat. He needed to give it permission to drop its guard, to help it understand viscerally that this response was no longer needed.

It was important that Tony began reinterpreting not only the big picture, but his individual thoughts as they arose in the moment. Every time he had a hopeless or dysfunctional thought about his symptoms, he labeled it as his anxious voice: an unreliable narrator that was drawn to catastrophe but had no basis in reality. He let that voice pass, and instead embraced a more valid and functional interpretation.

Tony needed to make adjustments to his behavior as well. His social isolation was denying him the laughter, activity, and stress relief that his friends could bring, so he committed to gradually reintegrating himself into his group of friends—and being open with them about what he was going through. He also began to slowly reintroduce exercise, which he had stopped doing once his physical symptoms had gotten tough. Shortly after picking his jogging habit back up, he noticed improvements in his sleep and his overall mood. He had his landlord install an extra deadbolt lock on his door as additional security, which gave him confidence that he had actively reduced the risk of further break-ins. He incorporated several relaxation exercises and meditations into his sleep routine at night, got a white noise machine, and committed to putting his smartphone "to bed" forty-five minutes before he went to bed. He increased his time outdoors, which also helped his sleep.

Physical Symptoms, Disempowered

Tony's Thoughts	Detoxed
This has happened for months now. I'll never feel normal again.	This has happened because my body still believes it needs to be on guard. I am teaching it that it no longer has to be.
My friends probably think that I'm lame, faking, or flaking out.	We all need extra understanding at times. These are people that I care about and value, and they will give me understanding, just like I've given it to them in the past. That's what strengthens close relationships.
I bet my body is damaged and doesn't remember how to feel good.	Nothing is fundamentally damaged. Those symptoms are my body working properly in terms of what it thinks it needs to do. Once it understands it doesn't need to be on high alert anymore, it will let itself relax.
How will I ever go to that conference if I feel like this?	I am making progress every day, and by the time that conference comes, I will likely be back to feeling like myself. And if not, at least I have the tools in the moment to not be as bothered by my symptoms.
That doctor probably screwed up my tests.	Having nothing physically wrong with me makes sense, because these reactions are a normal response to an anxiety-provoking event.
I bet therapy won't help, and then what?	I am already seeing the difference from working on this, and I can make progress one step at a time. Lots of others have gone through this and have benefited from the techniques I am learning to use.
I'm never going to get a good night's sleep again.	I am discovering how to reset my body, and every day I am making progress that helps me sleep better.

It took only a couple of weeks for Tony's physical symptoms to improve dramatically. The mechanism that did it was powerful, but it wasn't magic. Tony had learned to reinterpret his physical sensations. Even before his symptoms abated altogether, they began to worry and bother him far less—which in turn lowered his anxiety, jump-starting the cycle that eventually led him to feeling like himself again.

Meditations for Your Moment

We've covered a lot of ways your mind interacts with your body, and there's no better way to explore these further than to experiment with different types of meditations.

If you're groaning, I understand. And if you've heard for years how you "should" meditate but always thought it sounded silly, or if you've done it before without liking it whatsoever, that's OK. It's just important to give it a fair chance, and I'm offering a variety of mindfulness meditation techniques here to help you get in touch with what's going on with your inner life. You're working on being a gentle, nonjudgmental observer.

A good time to try these, if you're new to meditation, is when you are ending your day, lying in bed. Start by getting as comfortable as possible in a place free of distractions. You need not push any of your thoughts away: Your thoughts may wander, and that is totally OK. Remember: At this stage, the goal is awareness of your thoughts, and your breathing.

BODY SCAN

Slow down your breath as you breathe in through your nose, and out through your mouth, spending longer on the exhale than the inhale. Hold a hand on your belly to feel it expand on the inhale. Begin paying attention to your body. Try to become a gentle, nonjudgmental observer of whatever your body is experiencing, from head to toe, and tell yourself that it is all OK—you are only going to notice it. What do you feel, and where? Hot or cold sensations? Tingling? Itching? Tension or pain? Numbness? Buzzing? Twitching or shaking? When you feel your attention wander to your to-do list, or whether you need to buy more pet food, notice that too. And gently bring your attention back to your breath, without judgment. Try to keep your breathing slow and steady. Do this for a few minutes, or even longer if you find it calming.

SAFE PLACE

Breathe in slowly through your nose, and out through your mouth. Spend longer on the exhale. Hold a hand on your belly to feel it expand on the inhale. Envision a place that feels purely safe to you. Perhaps it is a place you've been; maybe it's a place you've made up in your mind. No one can be there without your permission. What does it look like? Color? Indoor or outdoor? Are there animals? Trees? What temperature is it there? Now imagine the actual shelter that you take within this place. Envision it wrapping you in its cocoon, a blanket of peace and light. You are safe. What does it sound like there? Are there calm, peaceful smells? Relax each muscle group as you ease into this space mentally and trust it to keep you safe. Stay with it for a few minutes as you keep your breath slow and steady.

GET GROUNDED

This one is helpful for those who are prone to panic, and also for those re-experiencing something traumatic in their past. When that happens, your body tends to go back into fight, flight, or freeze mode just as it did when you experienced the trauma for the first time. When your mind replays the traumatic experience, your body may believe it's truly back in that experience. Grounding yourself returns you to the mental and physical experience of this current moment, reestablishing your safety. It gives you a sense of being solid, secure, and in touch with your surroundings.

Pay attention to your breath and begin to slow it down, in through your nose, and out through your mouth. Spend longer on the exhale. Hold a hand on your belly to feel it expand on the inhale. Then use any of the following tools to remind yourself of where you are in the moment.

- Notice one thing in the room that is unmoving and focus on it as you breathe.
- Notice and name four things in the room, letting them anchor you and orient you to where you are.
- Pay attention to how your body comes into contact with the chair, bed, or floor, and how solid that feels.
- Listen to the sound of your breath, and the background sounds of the room or area around you.
- Put your hands gently together and notice how they feel to each other.
- Notice the way your clothes feel on your body.
- If you're mentally reexperiencing a trauma, visualize yourself—or the person hurt in the trauma you witnessed—safe and out of danger. (If that person has passed away, it still can be helpful to engage with the thought that they are no longer

in danger, that the traumatic moment is far behind, and that nothing can hurt them again. Many people find help in conceptualizing the person as being at peace.) Repeat as long as you need to.

SELF-COMPASSION

Giving meditation a try is a way of being kind to yourself, telling yourself that you—right here, right now—are worthy of space and time. In fact, meditation and self-compassion go hand in hand—and so let's try a meditation that concentrates on this.

Place your hands over your heart this time, and begin to notice your breath. Breathe in slowly through your nose and relax your body as you breathe out through your mouth. Take more time with the exhale than the inhale. Choose some of the following phrases to focus on and say to yourself, either out loud or silently, or go through them all one by one.

I can extend to myself the kindness that I extend to others.

I can learn to live with compassion and forgiveness for myself.

I deserve love.

I deserve peace in my heart and mind.

When I am kind to myself, I add kindness to the universe.

I deserve safety.

Life is not always easy, but I have strength within me that expands enough to make room for struggle.

I can make mistakes and keep trying in life, as we are all imperfect.

We are all on our own paths, and mine matters just as much as anyone else's.

When you feel your mind wander, give yourself compassion about that too. *My mind goes in its own direction sometimes. That's OK. I will keep reminding myself to be kind to it.*

Approaching Things Differently: Repetitive, Soothing Behavior

If you find that meditating (or trying to meditate) ends up making you more anxious, don't be hard on yourself. Focus instead on what your body feels like in an activity that is repetitive and soothing, like walking, doodling, or dancing while listening to music (even at your desk). If you are a fidgeter, consider a soothing sensory item to allow your mind to find calm even while your body is being stimulated: the notorious fidget spinner, squishy ball, slime, or shaking a snow globe and watching it settle. Some people even find repetitive cleaning activities a soothing way to engage themselves and focus on their breath. (I wish I were one of them.)

Reinterpreting and reframing your physical experience

By changing the narrative, you change your body's reaction—which helps your thoughts calm down, and fundamentally changes how you feel.

1 **STOP** yourself in the moment when your mood takes a dip or your thoughts become negative. Notice where in your body you feel it. What story are you telling yourself about what that means? Is there a gentler, less judgmental story that would be more functional?

2 **FOCUS** on those parts of your body during a breathing exercise or a mindfulness meditation. Envision the tension or discomfort leaving those parts of your body. Where applicable, try a physical exercise to help, like rolling your neck, stretching your arms, wiggling your fingers, or lying on the floor.

3 **CONSIDER** whether changes are needed in your overall habits. When does your body feel at its best? At its worst? Spend the next couple of days observing it. What are you willing to do differently?

3

You Hold On When You Need to Let Go

ACROSS HISTORY, IN VARIOUS LANGUAGES, human beings have created metaphors for carrying mental burdens: the albatross around your neck, the weight upon your shoulders, your heavy heart. Even the word "baggage" says it well: Most of us have some mental weight we feel forced to drag around on a daily basis. It preoccupies us and makes us feel sluggish. It sabotages our progress in life, preventing us from seeing the fullest picture of our potential, diminishing our hopes for the future.

Is there something significant you aren't letting go of? And if so, what's keeping you hanging on?

We often carry things that extend our burden, accumulating extra weight over time. Too many worries and mental checklists. And perhaps too much of the heavier stuff too: regrets, fears, and shame. It can be so hard to recognize our opportunities to let go.

One common burden we saddle ourselves with is obvious by now: our constant bickering with our thoughts. You've learned quite a bit about freeing yourself from that struggle once it tries to overtake you, but what about choosing not to enter that struggle in the first place? In ACT, that's referred to as "dropping the rope": extracting yourself from the tug-of-war with your thoughts by refusing to play along anymore. Rather than wear yourself out trying to overpower the enemy at the other end of the tug-of-war rope, you realize that you can let go. You get to choose whether or not to pick up that rope—in this case that struggle with your thoughts.

Monique and the Spectrum of Worry

Sometimes we don't want to let go because we think we shouldn't. We have anxious thoughts that we willingly grant long-term space in our brains because we believe that we *need* to be worrying about them. But worrying is a spectrum, and there is always a point at which it begins to do more harm than good, ceasing to be functional.

Take Monique, a sixty-two-year-old who had a history of anxiety. One particular week I saw her, she was debilitated by fears about the outcome of some medical tests. Unsurprisingly, she could not "talk herself out of" these fears, because the rational possibility remained that she did have a significant health condition. Since the worries could be true, Monique equated letting go of her negative thoughts with being in denial. To her, that meant being naïve and unprepared for a realistic potential threat.

What ideas are you engaging in a tug-of-war with?

Maybe it's not just your anxious thoughts, but it's your one-upmanship with your brother, your hope that your boss will finally give you the praise (or raise) you deserve, or the idea that you should absolutely lose those five extra pounds. In so many struggles, the struggle itself is the losing. Choosing to engage in the struggle guarantees that you'll sacrifice something significant, depleting yourself of mental and physical energy that could have been used to nourish yourself. It's just not worth it: The battle will be a chronic, permanent stalemate that seriously drains you in the process. Learning which areas of your life are needless tug-of-wars grants you the mental space and emotional freedom to save yourself from a lifetime of rope burn.

So Monique and I established a spectrum of what worry looked like. (Yup, we drew a picture.) We needed to determine the line between which thoughts to engage with and which Monique needed to grant herself permission to let go of. At the mild, functional end of the worry spectrum, Monique's negative thoughts allowed her to make a *plan*. They afforded her a sense of control, and she was genuinely better off for acknowledging this low-end worry. She could become more educated about her situation, compiling a list of potential questions for her doctor. She could do some *brief* research (no 2 a.m. Google black holes!) about treatments for the potential diagnosis. The low-end worries also motivated her to call a friend who was a supportive listener and always helped her calm down. So, these low-end worries we could accept: They increased her strength and preparedness, and increased her insight into her situation.

Now she had a plan—questions for her doctor, opening up to a friend, and educating herself on the basics. But beyond that point, at a certain mark on our worry spectrum, it became clear which thoughts were thoroughly unhelpful. They gave her no new insight or information. She was not using them to enhance or clarify her plan, or making herself any more prepared for the possibility of this diagnosis. Instead she was ruminating on those same anxiety-inducing thoughts over and over again. These thoughts were pretty obvious once she was willing to look. (*My life will never be the same! I'm certain the results are bad! It's all downhill from here!*) They made her feel worse, diminished her preparedness, and increased her dread. When she learned to label those thoughts as unhelpful and let them pass without holding on to them, she regained control over her situation.

Determining Which Thoughts Are "Worth" Worrying About

In times of significant stress, it's important to observe the different types of thoughts you're having, even if they're all related to the same general worry. You must recognize your own point on the spectrum of helpful versus unhelpful. (It's kind of like that Supreme Court justice's definition of pornography: You'll know it when you see it.) Summon the courage to release the thoughts that are redundant, dysfunctional, exaggerated, or unduly catastrophic—*even if there is some truth in them*. It may help to write down a concrete plan for handling the threat first, and then when you find your negative, anxious thoughts returning, ask yourself these two questions:

- Is this thought adding insight? Is it helping me clarify the plan?
- Is this thought increasing my preparedness or strength?

If the answer to both of these is no, then the thought is on the excess worry/not useful end of the spectrum. Treat it just as you would a thought that is inaccurate. It is similarly dysfunctional. Recognize the thought for what it is: an itch that can be breathed through and let go of. ("Hi, Anxious Thought. I see you there. Look, I'm aware that this fear could come true, but I've made a plan. I'll be flexible and adjust as needed. You're not teaching me anything—you're a heckler. But I know you'll pass on your own eventually. I'm going to focus on calming my breath and body for now.")

The Thoughts
Behind the Thoughts

What You're Telling Yourself	Why It's Inaccurate
Something is wrong with me because I have anxious thoughts.	Occasional anxious thoughts are natural for everyone.
I won't ever get better.	By reading this book, you're taking proven science-based steps to change things.
These thoughts won't ever go away.	That's technically true, but by detoxing them of their ability to stick, they lose much of their power to bother you.
I can't handle this.	You can, and you will. Your thoughts are never bigger than you are. You possess the ability to let them pass through you, and always will.
I am broken.	Your thoughts haven't broken anything in you; they don't possess that power on their own. And now that you are taking steps to address negative thoughts in a healthier way, they have even less power over you.

When the Thoughts Keep Coming Back

Opting out of the tug-of-war may feel draining in itself. You might be thinking, *But how exhausting for me to have to drop the rope, over and over again!* As we've established, relating differently to your thoughts is a process that takes practice, and it won't come magically overnight. Important things are happening every time you try, though. Each time you practice acknowledging your thought, labeling it, breathing through it, and letting it pass, you are creating new brain pathways that make it more automatic to think this way next time. Hey, you are growing new synapses! So even if it still feels tough, that doesn't mean you aren't making progress.

I know it can be discouraging when the thoughts keep coming back in the same anxious way. So watch for the thoughts about the thoughts—we call them meta-cognitions—that are dysfunctional.

Lauren and the Unchangeable Mother

"I just wish my mother was kinder," my client Lauren said after describing a particularly harrowing visit with her mom, Sharon, who made passive-aggressive comments to Lauren, her partner, and their daughter about the nit-pickiest of things, from their clothing and grammar to the amount of food they ate.

This had always been Sharon's way. She was often critical and harsh, and yet she could also be funny and interesting, with occasional surges of generosity that kept Lauren from cutting ties completely. Still, having visits like this was a downer, and Lauren sat in my office bemoaning the fact that her mother couldn't see how hurtful her comments were and change her behavior.

I gently reminded Lauren that this had been her wish all her life. And yet the only person capable of granting this wish—Sharon—was nowhere to be found in the therapy room. (She was probably barking at some poor waiter at that very moment.) And clearly it was not a wish that Sharon had ever shared. Years of attempts at heart-to-heart talks and adjusting Lauren's own behavior had never managed to budge Sharon's. Sharon tended toward cynicism and negativity, and she saw it as a realistic, appropriate way to handle an unjust world. Of course, she had the ability to change—if she so chose. But whether Sharon chose this was out of Lauren's control, as she had shown repeatedly, without exception, for decades. This wish wasn't likely to be granted, and Lauren needed to let go.

Letting Go of Unrealistic Expectations of Others

What Lauren *did* have control over was how she chose to incorporate her mother—the real one, not the fantasy one—into her life. She had the ability to set boundaries that worked for her and her family, to plan visits in ways that minimized the damage, and to protect herself emotionally by readjusting her expectations. She had the capability (and the responsibility) to make sure that the family that she had built with her partner and their daughter was not hurt by Sharon. And Lauren had the power to make sure that her mother's negative voice did not become her own.

But oh, how difficult it can be to relinquish the fantasy of having control over another person's behavior! And if you're particularly competent in other areas of life, then you're used to getting results, and will be tempted to keep trying harder. If it's someone you love, you may overpersonalize that individual's behavior, thinking it reflects directly upon you.

So letting go often involves accepting that other people may indeed make judgments. Yes, you may sometimes be blamed for the behavior of others who are close to you: guilt by association. But that is not a reason to keep depleting yourself trying to control something you can't control. We must learn to respect our own autonomy and that of others, even when we don't like their choices—and we also must learn to accept other people's right to make their own judgments, even when they make us uncomfortable. We are all our own people.

When the person you're hoping to change is your parent, as with Lauren, you probably overidentify with their opinion of you. This can trap you into chronically trying for their approval and acceptance—when in reality you need to be cultivating ways to better accept yourself.

Again, we are all our own people. And by letting go of unrealistic expectations of others, we let ourselves relinquish some serious baggage. We lighten the weight we are toting around, gaining more strength for ourselves. We free up our hands to carry the things we genuinely want to carry—and that we have some control over.

Lauren, Freed

At first, Lauren found that letting go of her hope that her mother would become kinder felt like giving up. Why *shouldn't* she hope for a better outcome with her mother? But she soon realized that the better outcome to strive for didn't involve changing Sharon—that had proven to be virtually impossible. The better outcome involved Lauren being more realistic and proactive in how she handled Sharon's visits. She learned that there were certain things she just would not bring up with her mother, because they invariably led to criticism. She cultivated more "safe" topics (certain television shows they shared an interest in) and activities (she purchased a membership for her family and Sharon at the zoo near Sharon's house) that would take Sharon away from the usual hot topics and settings that led most to criticism. She grew more assertive about ending conversations that had turned unkind, and practiced responses that helped this along: "We can agree to disagree," "I'll take that into consideration, but let's move on." She communicated frequently with her partner and her child about how the visits felt, and adjusted the frequency according to their needs. And most of all, she learned to disempower and let pass the voice that said her mother's criticism was somehow an accurate representation of how things really were.

Five Things You Can Start to Let Go of Right Now

In my years of working with clients, I've seen a wide array of mental burdens that people struggle to let go of, or even to realize they're holding on to. It's striking, though, how similar themes crop up again and again. Are you choosing to sabotage yourself by choosing to carry these common burdens?

PAST MISTAKES: We all screw up, and it's natural to have feelings about it. The problem with "if only" is it can't lead to action. On the other hand, the path you took is what's real, known and true, and it led you to where you are right now, with a wide-open future you *can* impact—in a way you can't ever impact your past.

Maybe you carry so much regret about not doing better in school that you don't ever bother exploring new career options. Or maybe you're so rueful of "wasting" your thirties on a dysfunctional relationship that you falsely believe it is too late to find someone new.

Don't let regrets skew your thinking so much that you miss the path forward. You don't have to let go of your past entirely if you don't want to. It gives you insight into who you are, and you can find meaning in the "if only"s. We'll talk more about this in Chapter 7, but the more you open your eyes to what your past has given you, and how it can be meaningful in a positive way, the more you can let go of its burden. You can even embrace it as motivation. "If only" can be altered to accept what is done, let go of regret, and be more insightful moving forward.

HOW THINGS "SHOULD" BE: Accepting that life isn't fair doesn't mean giving up the fight for justice, or believing that you shouldn't try to exert autonomy when you can. Instead, it means focusing on what you can control—and releasing yourself from your constant battle with what you can't. Protests, petitions, marches, and even voting are effective precisely because individual people recognized that although they alone couldn't change something completely, they could contribute to a changing tide. Your workplace culture may be dysfunctional, but you can live out your own values with your individual actions and interactions, adding incremental positivity. Your child's school may have policies you don't agree with, but you can have honest and nuanced discussions with your child about how to navigate a rule system that you have objections to, which helps them grow. And you may not be able to change a person's cruel behavior, but you can act in ways that put goodness back into the world, making their behavior more of an outlier.

With events that you have zero control over, what would it be like to accept those realities but find beauty or wonder somewhere within them, instead of struggling against them? It's like that Mr. Rogers quote, originally addressed to children watching frightening news on TV: "Look for the helpers." There are always people who will choose to help—no matter how dark the moment—and they bring with them a little bit of light.

YOUR PAST VISION OF YOUR FUTURE SELF: The concept of mourning extends beyond grief over the loss of someone we love. We also mourn missed expectations, the loss of things we had anticipated would happen but never did. You may have carried around many visions of your future self: what kind of person you'd be, what kind of lifestyle or partner you'd have. Maybe you expected X number of children, with Y personalities or Z abilities, or a certain kind of home or professional or educational status. It's rare that our lives turn out exactly as we had pictured. There is beauty in learning to bend and grow with these altered expectations, but let's be real: There is discomfort too. And often full-on pain, which we may try to block, avoid, or deny.

Is there something you need to let yourself mourn, in order to let go and move forward?

Your grief may be even more stark: Perhaps the loss of a loved one really did tear apart the life you had, or an injury, illness, or disability has changed your physical capabilities, or threatens to cut short your own life. Maybe an unexpected financial or professional setback has removed the material comfort you always assumed you would have.

Moving forward involves being willing to let go of the exact vision we have carried. Or the possibility that things can still be the way they were (or how we wanted them to be). Our refusal to let go may start as self-coping, but past a certain point it becomes a hindrance. What growth can you open yourself up to by letting go of this vision of yourself you've been carrying for too long?

GOALS THAT NO LONGER SUIT YOU: You may have changed your mind a lot about who you were between age eight and sixteen, but not nearly as much between thirty-six and forty-four. Stability is good, of course—but adulthood's quicker passage of time can lead us to hold on to goals and beliefs about ourselves long past their expiration date. Are you clinging to something that suited the 2006, 2009, or 2019 version of you, but not the you who's alive right now?

We'll talk details of goal-setting in Chapter 9, but for now, ask yourself: Am I holding on to a certain goal that is no longer serving me? Does it represent who I really want to be, in my current reality, or does it represent an outdated fantasy? Have I allowed myself to fully accept the me that I really am, rather than the Possible Future Me that Past Me was hung up on?

That's right. Past You and Future You both ignore something important. What is missing?

Present You

Past You's estimate of Future You likely does not equal the correct, true, and real version of Present You. The math just doesn't work.

Present You may be a whole other person altogether. And that is absolutely, positively OK.

Present You deserves to have goals, activities, and values that reflect your true self, not some outdated daydream of a person who no longer exists.

PHYSICAL ARTIFACTS: Expired fantasies of Future You can intrude in physical ways too: the dresses that haven't fit in years, the cool lamp you were always going to fix, the workout gear that turned out to be scratchy and uncomfortable but that you said you'd just deal with because you were going to learn to love exercise so much. Or the marble cheese board that you've never once used (but if you ever had a cocktail party for 150 people would be an absolute must).

Research has shown that clutter is associated with a higher stress response, especially among women. The weight of clutter takes up significant mental space, whether it's boxes of things you just had to save that you never open, or the daily time lost in a hunt for your keys amid the disaster that is your entryway table. It can be quite intimidating to get rid of "stuff," which is why home organizing has become such a lucrative industry.

But when you hold on to burdensome physical items only because Past You thought that its version of Future You should use them, would need them, could fix them, or would like them, then you are doing a terrible disservice to Present You. Or when you refuse to deal with that stack of bills or decide what to do with that box of dishware from Grandma, you're weighing Present You down with mental clutter as well as physical mess.

And that's not fair.

(Because, not to play favorites, but I like Present You best of all.)

Approaching Things Differently: Gentle Nudges

By this point, you may know what it is you need to let go of, but you may feel like it keeps coming back, thought by thought. Occasionally this cycle gets so fierce as to feel insurmountable. I had a client who called this "getting wrapped around the axle." This is particularly common for thoughts that induce a strong physical reaction, because the physical reaction keeps them around, making them stick. So, as a first step, use the tools from Chapter 2 when these thoughts keep pummeling you.

And take heart that the more you practice these techniques and the less the thoughts begin to stick, the less you will notice them returning. More important, the less they will bother you when they do. Remember, the goal here is not to avoid the thoughts. The goal is to learn to tolerate them, and not care about them as much anymore.

But if the cycle still feels too intense or bothersome to make headway, here are some additional ways to give the thoughts a nudge.

WRITE DOWN THE THOUGHTS — COMPLETELY UNCEN-SORED: Let them have their say. Then fold them up and tuck them away to be dealt with later.

DESIGNATE A "WORRY TIME": Specifically carve out this time, perhaps during your commute or as you take a walk. Commit to nudging anxious thoughts aside until then. ("I hear you, worry. I will get to you, but it is not your time yet. At five o'clock you will have my attention.")

IMAGINE YOUR THOUGHTS AS AN ITEM ON YOUR TO-DO LIST FOR A LATER TIME: Now picture yourself "clocking out" of the worry workday, giving yourself permission to have the night off.

SWITCH UP YOUR SENSES: Change rooms, put on some music, or smell something you like (aromatherapy allows your brain to press the reset button and shift its attention). Do something that makes you laugh. Doodle or color. Drink something hot or wrap yourself in a heavy blanket. Soak your feet. Go out in the cold or warm air.

DO THE MATH: Pretend you have a menu with two different options of worry sizes: the entrée (perhaps seven full days of worry about an upcoming event), or the side dish (just two days). Think about the limits of your appetite for worry. Now embrace your choice: Mindfully say "no, thanks" to your worry when it is repeatedly offered, until two days before the event.

USE YOUR BODY AS A RESET BUTTON: Inhale as you raise your hands above your head, then release your arms and propel them downward like a windmill as you exhale fully and assertively, saying "I am letting this go." Repeat as needed.

Dropping the rope

The better you can identify what you have learned to carry that is no longer serving you day in and day out, the more you free up your mental energy for the person that you truly want to be, here and now.

1 **VISUALIZE** your body floating, moving forward through life. What weighs it down? What tugs at you in ways that don't feel good: roles you play that don't let you be yourself? Regrets you've played tug-of-war with for years? Past expectations of yourself, or the expectations of others? Anger that the world isn't fair? Too much material "stuff"? A suboptimal health habit? A home environment or relationship that doesn't suit you?

2 **IMAGINE** the future you want—its shape, color, texture, and size. How will all of those weights be incorporated into it? Which won't be, and what can you commit to letting go of?

3 **ENVISION** moving forward toward your chosen future in a mindful way. What you don't want to let go of, reframe as providing you experience and opportunity for growth. Imagine how these former weights add to your insight, depth, strength, and empathy. Then draw a picture that symbolizes this more complex but more insightful and beautiful future. Commit to being mindful of this picture as you move forward, taking small steps each day. And commit to practicing this future, taking small, mindful steps each day toward living it.

PART II

Your Moment

"There is a crack, a crack in everything.
That's how the light gets in."

LEONARD COHEN, "ANTHEM"

4
You're Blind to Your Blind Spots

5
You Run from Discomfort

4

You're Blind to Your Blind Spots

WE ALL HAVE BLIND SPOTS in how we perceive and make sense of the world. ("My child would never bully anyone!" "*I'm* not yelling. *You're* yelling!" "I broke the rule because I had a good reason, but no one else should be allowed to!")

We all see life through our own lenses, but we often don't realize how blurry, scratched, or skewed they are.

No one's lens is perfect, and we all use shortcuts to interpret the world, which our brains desperately need. Cognitive psychologists call these "heuristics"—the mental groupings we make to streamline our thought processes, allowing us to categorize and make decisions quickly. Even if you've never seen a particular breed of dog before, you'll probably be able to tell it right away from a ferocious, wild wolf—precisely because your brain has learned to extrapolate. Having quick ways to organize the gazillion pieces of data that bombard us each day reduces our stress and our energy output. Can you imagine how burned-out our mental computers would be if we had to do these calculations from scratch every time we encountered something new? Thank goodness we have some help.

Even paying selective attention helps us at times. If you are in the market for a new car, you'll probably start noticing different makes and models to help you figure out what you want, even if you normally couldn't tell a Camaro from an El Camino. If your two kids need orthodontia, you'll suddenly start noticing people's teeth.

Plus, almost everyone exaggerates or rounds off complicated edges once in a while. Maybe it's for simplicity, clarity, or just because we want a better punchline for a story. These behaviors don't always cause harm, and they can at times help us cope.

But when the oversimplifications misfire and become a habit, you've got danger—especially if you are already prone to negative, anxious thinking. You'll feel more threatened and pessimistic about virtually everything: yourself, your loved ones, and your future. You'll be led into a trap without even realizing it.

By discovering and acknowledging your blind spots, you can counteract them—rise above your faulty lenses and keep them from leading you astray. It all starts with awareness—which lets you identify these categories of dysfunctional thoughts that you may never have realized were trapping you. Only then can you learn to treat them like other negative thoughts: labeling them, defusing them, and letting them pass.

Are you ready to learn the most common ways our lenses are distorted?

You've already begun to learn how to recognize your anxious thoughts as unreliable narrators.

But these other skewed-lens thoughts may not even appear to you as distorted (yet). You might even assume they are coming from your objective, reasoning mind. And that's a big problem. To recognize these patterns, you'll need to look closely not only at how you think, but how you speak and write. Remember: How you say things doesn't just reflect how you think about them. It affects how you think about them too.

ALL-OR-NONE THINKING: Whether we call it all-or-none thinking, splitting, dichotomous thinking, absolutism, either/or, or black-or-white thinking, this brand of mental trap is ubiquitous. A majority of my clients tend toward it at some point or another, no matter what they're in therapy for, and it seems pervasive in the way that many people talk about their days. It's particularly common in individuals who have frequent relationship conflicts (or are terrified of them), people who have deficits in their self-esteem, and people who are dealing with binge-eating or substance abuse. All-or-none thinking contributes to procrastination, grudges, and self-sabotage. Even more serious, all-or-none thinking intensifies the chokeholds of anxiety and depression, adding hopelessness and helplessness to the mix.

It's so damaging because it goes directly against the kind of *cognitive flexibility* that helps us cope with negativity in our lives. It ignores the middle ground where beauty, hope, complexity, and interest (and actual reality) tend to live. It drastically reduces our options and constricts us, narrowing our world.

So, let's be clear: You must always, 100 percent, absolutely and completely avoid all-or-none thinking. (Kidding!)

But you most certainly must be honest with yourself about whether you engage in it. Does a small setback make you feel like all is lost? Do you frequently have "the worst day ever"? Does one encounter with a bad apple of a human lead you quickly down the path of "people suck"?

That's not reality. So why create that world for yourself to live in?

Of course, sometimes all-or-none words are completely valid and make perfect sense to use. (It's safe to say I will *never* become a world champion skeet shooter.) But let's be honest: All too often, they're a shortcut to a negative, dysfunctional trap.

The Usual Suspects

ALL-OR-NONE WORDS THAT TRAP YOU:

"Always" or **"Never"**

Escalating arguments and accusations: "You're always late!" "You never do anything nice for me!"

Diminishing hope for the future: "I never catch a break." "I always get taken advantage of." "This will never improve."

Stereotyping and removing the benefit of the doubt: "People will always hurt you if you let them." "Men always only care about sex."

"Everything" or **"Total"**

Catastrophizing setbacks: "My life totally sucks." "Everything's going wrong."

Removing motivation: "My house is a total pigsty. I give up." "Everything ends up a disappointment."

"Ruined"

Exaggerating blame or shame: "You ruined this evening for me!" "Oh, no. I ruined everything!"

Obscuring a solution: "This project is now ruined. There's no point in fixing it." "It's all ruined. And we don't have time to start over, so we're screwed!"

"Can't"

Deceiving you into helplessness and hopelessness: "I can't handle this." "We can't recover from this."

Creating an excuse for self-sabotage: "I can't do anything right." "I can't figure this out. Screw it!"

"Everyone" or **"No one"**

Entrenching a "me versus them" mentality: "No one cares about me." "Everyone's out for their own needs."

Viewing the world more negatively: "No one keeps their word in this day and age." "Everyone's so rude on the subway."

"Anymore"

Idealizing the past at the expense of the future: "People just don't take the time for others anymore." "I used to be respected at work, but not anymore."

Entrenching a fear of change: "I just can't seem to figure things out anymore." "I used to have it all together, but not anymore."

All-or-None Behavior

Once your thinking is sabotaged by an all-or-none mind-set, your behavior easily follows suit. Do you recognize yourself in either of these examples?

You were supposed to be avoiding processed food but you've eaten a bunch of chips. So you decide all is lost and you might as well finish off the bag, and then you eat a sleeve of Girl Scout cookies too. This leaves you feeling even more down on yourself, and you decide there's just no way you're going to the gym later.

Or, your partner has had to work late four times this month, and you are majorly annoyed. An argument begins, and instead of being specific about how those four times have affected you and suggesting a plan to move forward, you immediately put your partner on the defensive by blurting out that they "always" choose work over you and "never" consider your feelings and that their job is "ruining" your life together.

NEGATIVITY BIAS: Another blind spot that leads to toxic self-talk is the negativity bias. Personalities show wide variability across the optimism/pessimism dimension. There are the glass-half-full people, the glass-half-empty people, and an entire spectrum in between. But the vast majority of us, it turns out, are prone to accepting negative things more easily than positive things, even if we are generally optimistic. We react to negativity more strongly and quickly—our brain's alarm system, the amygdala, makes sure of this—and we are less able to be convinced to change our interpretation later on.

This negativity bias is evolutionary. Tens of thousands of years ago, if someone in your tribe had veered a wee bit homicidal, your survival depended on your ability to detect it. But in modern life, this negativity bias can tip things in a pretty dark direction, even when (or especially when!) there's no homicidal neighbor to worry about. It means that insults typically have a more potent sticking ability than praise; bad news affects your mood more than good news; threats sink in more viscerally than reassurance—regardless of the significance of the information. Have you ever had a performance review where the solitary negative comment is what's still with you two days later? Perhaps you scored high overall, but that single minor criticism is the first thing that comes to mind when you tell your partner how your review went.

The more you understand that negative information carries unduly heavy weight, the more you can remind yourself that your lens is unreliable when you interpret this information. So you become better able to label it as inaccurate, breathe through it, and let it pass, without lending it the credence of sticking around and affecting your judgment.

CONFIRMATION BIAS: Confirmation bias can be just as problematic. We've all probably had the experience of being in an argument with someone who sees only what they want to see, ignoring any evidence against it. (Funny how everyone *else* does this, right?) The reality is, we are all prone to confirmation bias: seeking out and favoring evidence that supports our beliefs, and assuming that is the only valid evidence out there.

If you're feeling frustrated that your partner's not doing enough around the house, you may notice only that they didn't take out the trash, and ignore the half hour they spent doing laundry. If you're in a rut with negative self-talk saying you're socially inept, then you'll remember only the time you stumbled in conversation at the party, rather than the people who liked your joke or the rounds of small talk that went just fine. Unfortunately, this magnifies your social anxiety for the next time you go out. Worse yet, confirmation bias can keep you choosing behaviors that are misguided, because you notice only the "evidence" that your decisions are working, rather than the potential that another path might be better.

Turned outward rather than inward, confirmation bias can magnify hate, resentment, and jealousy. If you believe something negative about a group of people, you are more likely to pay attention only to stories that further your negative stereotype, justifying—in your mind at least—your bias further.

STAKES VERSUS ODDS—ANXIETY'S BAD MATH: Anxiety creates yet another blind spot for us: the tendency to view the *stakes* of something happening as far more important than the *odds*. In other words, your brain focuses on the negative effects of something happening more than the likelihood that it actually will. And you're often unable to reason yourself out of it. Why are so many people so much more frightened of a plane crash versus a car crash, despite the fact that the latter is far more likely? The stakes for a plane crash are far higher. A plane crash will likely lead to your death, whereas most car accidents let you emerge from your vehicle in one piece, ready to copy down insurance policy numbers.

And guess what? An anxious brain isn't attracted to insurance policy numbers. Nor to a rational explanation of statistical odds, or reassurance of the millions of passenger trips each year that are completely without incident. No, an anxious brain wants to visualize mayhem, disaster, and death. OK, it doesn't necessarily *want* to visualize that—but it can't help doing so. An anxious brain is attracted to catastrophe like I am to tzatziki.

So your brain gets hijacked by stakes that are particularly scary to visualize. You may "know" that just because the stakes are scary doesn't mean the odds are likely of it happening (*I get it—plane crashes are rare*). But your rational brain has a very tough time winning this battle, because the visual is so terrifying and attention-grabbing.

How can you win? Don't empower that catastrophized visual of the fiery crash. Neutralize it. Breathe through it. Label it. Use the tools of Chapter 1 to brand it an unreliable narrator, a cheesy horror film on late-night TV that will eventually go to commercial. It's an itch of your anxious mind that does not have to be scratched, a mental hiccup that will pass on its own.

Embracing Uncertainty

But let's be clear: Refusing to catastrophize is not the same thing as going into denial. People who are prone to anxiety are desperate for absolute certainty. They want the magic genie to tell them that there is precisely a 0.00000000000 percent chance their plane will crash, that the risk is truly nil. Those are the holy grail odds that feel truly reassuring to someone whose anxiety is spiraling about the stakes of something.

But increasing your ability to tolerate distress involves increasing your ability to tolerate uncertainty. Pretty much anything carries more than a 0.00000000000 percent chance of happening. I mean, in theory, a live salamander could pop out of the next page at this very moment. Seriously, I really can't give you absolute certainty that it won't, especially if you live in Florida.

You may want reassurance of a total lack of risk, just as someone with OCD wants a total removal of their intrusive thoughts. But that can't happen and shouldn't be the goal. *Living comes with risk*. Reading this book comes with risk. Sitting on your chair comes with risk. You may want a guarantee that you will forever be "safe" in doing the things you fear: revealing your true emotions to a loved one, going to the doctor, asking for a raise, booking an adventure, or starting up a conversation. But there are no true guarantees. And you can take that either as a reason not to fully engage with living, or just as a fact of life that is part of the whole bargain.

In the case of OCD, the only way forward is learning to coexist with your intrusive thoughts, which you can do by neutralizing them. In the case of anxiety about risk, the path forward is the same—learning to coexist with your uncertainty, and to accept and tolerate it, which neutralizes it. Don't give in to yet another urge to view things in all-or-none terms. Life has uncertainty, and you can breathe through that and learn to coexist with it, using your mindfulness techniques. You can remind yourself that in uncertainty also lie opportunity, freedom, and adventure.

COGNITIVE DISSONANCE: Perhaps you heard the phrase years ago in Intro Psych. But it looms large as another way that we blind ourselves to reality. We don't tend to love discomfort (a well-worn point by now), and so our brains try various ways to escape it. This means that when we have two thoughts that don't seem to fit together well, we tend to be quick to change one of them—even if it leads us astray.

Cognitive dissonance can make you lie to yourself. You'll change your interpretation of things, not to a more valid one, or one that's better aligned with your long-term well-being, but to what's simplest and most comfortable right then. You'll pick whichever one of the two dissonant ideas is "easiest" to change, creating a gaping blind spot.

This often creates false dichotomies, where you believe that two things are mutually exclusive when in reality they are not. You may needlessly force yourself to choose one or the other, ignoring that both can exist. I've seen this lead to plenty of false and damaging beliefs, like the ones listed here:

FALSE & DAMAGING BELIEF	CLAIMS
Kindness = Being a doormat	If you are a kind person, you will always put other people first and not stand up for yourself when you are being mistreated.
Loving someone = Getting along perfectly at all times	Being in a happy relationship means never having a conflict.
Mental health = Being free of difficult emotions	Being an emotionally healthy person means never feeling sad, mad, angry, or just occasionally "meh" for no particular or clear reason.
Being productive = Working all the time	Being a hard worker means never taking a real day off.
Being strong = Going it alone	Having emotional strength means never asking for help.
Intelligence = Having certainty about everything	Being a smart person means always knowing the answers.
Optimal parenting = Ignoring your own needs	Being a loving or good parent means never taking care of your own needs before those of your kids.
Attractiveness = Physical perfection	Being a desirable person means always being perfectly put together, or perfectly photographed.

FALSE & DAMAGING BELIEF	CLAIMS
Deserving love = Earning it through achievement	Being worthy of love is not a given, but instead comes from having done something to merit it.
Being a competent person = Never making mistakes	Missteps are shameful signs of weakness, rather than ways of learning and growing.
Being brave = Not being afraid	Courage means feeling no fear, instead of feeling fear and moving through it.

Grace and Things That Aren't as They Seem

Grace was twenty-seven and had been with Justin for eight years. She had developed a tremendous crush on him in college, and had gone on to—in the teasing words of her friends—"stalk" him until they were eventually in a relationship. Because he was her first-ever boyfriend, her love and admiration for him was powerful. She had envisioned soon into their relationship that she wanted to be with him forever. He dragged his feet with each new step of commitment: becoming monogamous, meeting each other's families, moving to the same city after graduation, living together, and most recently, getting engaged. Each time, Grace felt a jolt of triumph when he finally took the step she had so desperately wanted.

Two months into their engagement, something disturbing happened: Grace found evidence that Justin was not the person she thought he was. Not only was it clear he had been sleeping with other women for several years, but he had amassed thousands of dollars in gambling debt. When confronted, Justin denied having a gambling problem and claimed that the supposed affairs were all in Grace's head (despite solid evidence and the corroboration of a friend who had been too scared to say anything until Grace asked her point-blank). Grace was shattered, but of course did not want to be shattered. She wanted to marry this man—since the night she had first talked to him at a keg party.

Enter cognitive dissonance.

Grace had two conflicting, or dissonant, notions. The first was that it appeared that Justin was a dishonest, unfaithful person who had deceived Grace for years. The second was that Grace had spent her twenties trying to get this guy to commit to her. She had devoted so much energy to being a couple, planning their future together, and—finally—having her parents spend thousands of dollars in preparation for a wedding that was supposed to begin their happily married life.

These two ideas did not go together easily, and Grace's brain—like many of ours—could not handle the discomfort.

So it looked for a way out. The quickest way to get rid of dissonance between two things? Adjust one of them to no longer be true.

Clearly, Grace could not change that she had spent eight years in love with Justin, devoted to their lives together. She could not change that her parents had put a down payment on a swing band and thrown a lavish engagement party. She did not even *want* to change the fact that she still viewed him as the love of her life.

But she could change her interpretation of the other part—the apparent dishonesty. Maybe there was more to it. Maybe he hadn't really lied. Maybe the money was all a big misunderstanding. Maybe the emails weren't real. Maybe her friend was lying to her. Yes, maybe Justin was still a man worthy of her love. In this narrative, he was imperfect (wasn't everyone?), but he was still the right one for her. They had *not* been living a lie. She did not have to throw it all away. He had just made some mistakes, and she had misinterpreted.

If Grace simply adjusted the "Justin is dishonest" concept a bit, then there was no longer dissonance. She could still stay with this person to whom she had given her entire adult life. She could still believe that being with him was right, and that it meant what she thought it did. She could still live the life she had planned, on the surface at least.

It was by far the most soothing choice in the moment—even if in the long term, it was terrible for her.

There was no shortage of evidence that Justin was not worthy of Grace and would go on to break her heart over and over again. But the further Grace dug in her heels—a mentality increased by her fear of "losing her investment" in the relationship (the sunk-cost fallacy)—the harder it would be for her to ever get out. All the while, her brain would keep blinding her to what she so desperately needed to see.

So.

Are there unsettling truths you are blinding yourself to, to feel more comfortable in the present moment?

It's really time you looked at them.

Embracing Complexity

Recognizing your blind spots is only part of the solution. You need a path toward change, an alternative to thinking and behaving this way. As you observe yourself in a misguided thought, stop, take a breath, and attempt to step outside of it by labeling it as the trap that it is. Offer yourself an alternative perspective. It may be a gray area, a middle ground, the unpacking of a box, or a more nuanced landscape. Adding a visualization can help. Start thinking in terms of spectrums, axes, and gradations of color, to get away from the rigidity and oversimplification of the blind spot.

Having trouble with this mind-set shift? The harder it feels to get yourself out of the trap, the more valuable it will be to do so. And you can even catch yourself in your all-or-none thoughts about this process and practice counteracting them as a starting place. (Out: *If I've thought this way for thirty years, I'll never be able to change.* In: *This way of thinking is a serious habit of mine. But each time I catch myself in it—including now—I am growing stronger, making it a little less likely to happen the next time.*)

The Sunk-Cost Fallacy

I mentioned that part of Grace's distress came from the fact that she had spent all of her adult life with Justin. She had sacrificed a lot, and turned down innumerable opportunities that might have taken her in a different direction with a different partner, home, or career. She had chosen to invest instead in her life with Justin, which could have been a wonderful thing—had Justin been worthy of it.

The price of this investment was a *sunk cost* that Grace could never get back. The fallacy comes from believing that to honor this past cost, you must continue on a misguided path, as if that will somehow recoup your investment or make it "worth it." It's why you stay on hold with customer service for the tenth straight minute, all for a minuscule refund that you wouldn't have considered worth ten minutes in the first place. It's why you keep pouring money into a faulty appliance instead of cutting your losses and starting over with a new one. Though it's often cited in economic decisions, it applies very much to interpersonal ones like Grace's as well. She couldn't get those years back, and staying with Justin would just add to her wasted time. But in her mind, the investment somehow *wasn't* wasted if she just hung in there.

To counteract the sunk-cost fallacy, make a different calculation. Visualize the investment as something finalized, no matter what you choose next. It cannot be recouped. It is solidified. It is locked. This might make you feel helpless and regretful, but you still have power here. Because what *can* be recouped is any money/time/effort you would have chosen to invest *going forward*. You still have complete control over that. That's where you can start to balance the numbers. If you keep yourself stuck on the wrong path, you are increasing your loss over time. (Grace's parents' deposit on the wedding band is one thing, but it's nothing compared with the cost of a divorce—just as Grace's heartache would be magnified then as well. Continuing to lie to herself would only compound her future pain.)

Remember that your past investment was not in vain. It is not wasted if you choose to use it to know yourself better and be more insightful in the future. Those who have made some mistakes and used them to illuminate their blind spots have arguably gained more insight than those who never made the mistake in the first place.

DEPRESSED ATTRIBUTIONS: People who are prone to depression have blind spots of their own in how they perceive negative experiences, making the negativity even more sticky, according to research by Martin Seligman, building on the work of Aaron Beck. Specifically, depressed individuals tend to view negative experiences through an internal lens—meaning that they view them as their own personal fault, blaming themselves ("She didn't say hi to me because I am boring and unlikable") rather than neutral attributions ("We must have been too far apart for her to see me") or external ones ("Wow, she is rude"). Even with all things being equal and there being an objective explanation for something, a depressed person is more likely to have skewed judgment that puts the onus on themselves.

They are also more likely to take a negative thing that is specific and turn it into something global—applying it generally to everything. This is akin to the all-or-none pattern we've discussed. A minor round of setbacks becomes "the worst week ever"; a non-working microwave means "This place is a dump."

Finally, depressed folks are prone to the false belief that negative things will not improve. This is understandable, of course, because depression itself can feel so miserable that it's hard to step out of it enough to even imagine feeling OK. Part of its brutality is masking the recognition that the darkness can, and very likely will, lift in the future. Unfortunately, this leads very easily to hopelessness.

These attributions are emblematic of depression to the point where you might say, "Well, of course—thinking that way is what depression *is*." But these ways of thinking are not just symptoms of depression; they likely predate it as risk factors or even causes.

Catching yourself in this thinking (recognizing it, labeling it as an inaccurate blind spot, defusing yourself from it mindfully and not letting it stick as your reality) can help keep you from falling into a depressive rut.

DEFENSE MECHANISMS: Another way our blind spots damage us is through our defense mechanisms. Originally theorized by Sigmund Freud, whose legacy is far from perfect (what was with all that stuff about your mom?), but whose general ideas about unconscious motives were revolutionary, defense mechanisms come from our desire to protect ourselves from feeling bad. We *defend against* difficult feelings by trying to get their discomfort to go away.

You may have developed favorite defense mechanisms that you use again and again as coping strategies, attempting to hide from feelings you don't want to have or realities you don't want to deal with. But as with any trap, a defense mechanism has the potential to do far more harm than good. Do you recognize any of these in yourself?

DENIAL: You claim that a difficult feeling doesn't exist. "No, the breakup doesn't bother me at all. We weren't right for each other. End of story."

PROJECTION: You project your feelings on to someone else, trying to convince yourself that the other person is having them, not you. "I know you probably feel terrible about how poorly you've been treating me, being so mean all the time."

RATIONALIZATION: You latch on to a "rational" explanation for your behavior, rather than the real, emotional reason. "Of course I wasn't driving by my ex's house. I have a new app that shows me where the cheapest gas is, and it just so happens it was seventeen miles away and coincidentally by his house."

DISPLACEMENT: You redirect your uncomfortable feelings onto a "safer" target. Instead of screaming at your boss, you come home and unload on your partner because there are dishes on the counter, or you rage at someone in traffic.

SUPPRESSION/REPRESSION: This is denial on steroids. You bury a feeling or experience so deeply that it is virtually inaccessible to your conscious mind, but it is prone to eventually exploding out if you are triggered by something. This often happens with a trauma or extremely painful experience that you want to avoid reexperiencing.

REACTION FORMATION: You consciously take the opposite stand of uncomfortable feelings, like publicly crusading against something you're privately doing or feeling. Or being so lovey-dovey with your partner on social media that it makes your friends and family gag—when in reality, your relationship is falling apart.

The problem with defense mechanisms is twofold: not only do they not work very well (doing very little to get rid of your distress in the first place), but they also close your eyes to the reality of the situation, blocking you from finding a better path forward.

What Can We Do Instead?

Even Freud allowed us a little hope. *Sublimation* gives you the chance to turn your angst into something more beautiful and helpful to your well-being.

When you engage in sublimation, you channel your uncomfortable feelings into something progressive or creative, like the stand-up comedian who gains a new perspective on their difficult upbringing through making others laugh. Or the artist who processes their pain by putting it on a canvas. Or the formerly bullied runner who pounds the pavement, channeling their desire for revenge into the ability to revel in their own strength.

But I like to take this even farther than Freud did. Let's try applying sublimation not just to individual impulses, but to life in general.

What can you make of your tough stuff? Or more specifically, what will you *choose* to make of it? In all of our paths, there are experiences that don't fit our ideals: embarrassments, setbacks, emotions that feel like weaknesses, and incidents we wish we could do over. How can you turn those into something that matters in a positive way?

This is not masking reality; it is *seeing* it. It is being engaged with it, living it, and maybe even loving it—while growing it into something that works for you.

So many of us live our lives as Grace did: seeing only what is most comfortable to see. Or we trick ourselves into absorbing a skewed picture of reality, a flawed and dysfunctional vision that preys on our fears or oversimplifies the world into a flat, black-and-white place.

The lenses we use to see the world are ours alone. When we can devote some attention to examining our blind spots, those lenses become clearer and more accurate. By understanding your personal thought distortions—ones you undoubtedly share with many other people—you can label them as dysfunctional, allowing them to pass just as you have learned to do with other types of self-talk. By removing your blind spots, you may see things you didn't think you could handle, but by opening your mind and eyes to them, you learn that you can.

Truly owning the tough stuff in your life turns it into fuel to keep you going, adding nuance and depth to the big picture of your life. It takes creativity and vulnerability, and a change of perspective. Are you willing?

Engaging in this way of living is not the same thing as pretending that your heart isn't broken. Instead, to paraphrase D. H. Lawrence, it is understanding that there may be something truly beautiful and kaleidoscopic within the places where it cracked.

PRACTICE:

Recognizing and counteracting your blind spots to gain insight

Learning to acknowledge your personal blind spots, and their role in your daily life, will help you better label some of your negative thoughts as dysfunctional and let them pass. This lays the foundation for a more resilient mind-set.

1 **WRITE** down four potential areas of blind spots for you. Start with some of your insecurities or your strongest opinions. Or think of the negative self-talk that plagues you most: What blind spots might be there? List the costs and benefits: There are reasons you keep this skewed lens (convenience, simplicity, comfort), but there is also harm, to you and others.

2 **LABEL** the blind spots that you have determined are dysfunctional or misleading, and ask yourself how you could incorporate alternative evidence into the moment, perhaps by engaging in self-distancing. "Ben is really oversimplifying things here; there's a gray area that he needs to acknowledge." Or pretend you are a cross-examining attorney and the voice of the skewed lens is on the witness stand. Is that voice being untruthful? Glossing over things? Exaggerating? What damage is that voice causing?

3 **DEVELOP** a shortcut for combatting this type of thinking. (After all, the thinking arises from our need for shortcuts.) Come up with a quick, simple saying that directly refutes the skewed voice. Keep practicing it whenever you catch yourself slipping. ("There are multiple sides to things." "Jumping to conclusions doesn't help me." "I will keep my mind open.")

5

You Run from Discomfort

SOME ACT THERAPISTS I KNOW are very fond of Chinese finger traps, and even keep a drawer full of them. That's because these classic children's toys—woven, colorful bamboo tubes—make for a powerful metaphor. When you put your fingers in from each side of the tube, your fingers get stuck, and pulling them out won't free them. Struggle, curse, and yank all you want—the trap just gets tighter.

But take a breath and push your fingers slowly *inward*—in other words, don't try right away to escape your situation, but instead lean into it—and the trap now loosens enough that you get some space. The struggle becomes far less dire, and you are much less constricted and uncomfortable. Once you fully do this, you gain yourself enough wiggle room that you can get yourself out.

Uncomfortable feelings are like this, too.

Stress, worry, anger, sadness, boredom, guilt—all of them are inherently unpleasant. But although these feelings aren't comfortable, they still may be quite *useful*. Unlike our running commentary of thoughts, which can frequently be random or incidental, feelings are often more telling. They may represent a longer-term reaction to our thoughts having stuck, or be a warning sign that we are offtrack in our behavior. Feelings typically take longer to build than thoughts do, so they are more likely to have something underneath them worth examining. Many emotions have something important to tell us, if we don't immediately give in to the temptation to run away from them or tune them out.

In modern life, choosing not to run from our emotions is tough. We possess a skyrocketing number of tools to help us tune out our uncomfortable emotions. And our cultural norms have shifted in favor of doing anything, *anything*—including scrolling through photos of our cousin's sister-in-law's commute to work—to avoid our discomfort.

The problem is, the more we run from something, the less experience we gain in managing it.

As the saying goes, smooth seas never made a skilled sailor. Who do you want as your ship captain: the one who's never navigated through a storm in his or her life? Or the captain who's faced threatening, unpredictable gale-force winds and learned how to move through them? Who would you expect to be calmer and more competent when a storm comes?

Avoidance of discomfort only sensitizes us to it. It's a paradoxical trap: You grow accustomed to running from uncomfortable emotions, and the more you run from them, the more afraid of them you become, so you'll continue to run in the future. You also never learn what would have happened if you *hadn't* avoided the uncomfortable feelings or problems. Instead you become less equipped to handle them, but since the avoidance and distraction make you feel better briefly, the running is positively reinforced, and will likely become your coping mechanism of choice.

What Stories Do You Tell Yourself about Emotions?

Every family is different. And just as they all have different ways of eating, different definitions of "vacation," and different attitudes about religion (or Star Wars), they also have vastly different ways of handling emotion. Those habits and practices tend to be formative, sticking with you long after you're on your own. What did you witness growing up when it came to the experience of emotion? Might it be part of your story even now? Ask yourself this:

- How did my parents/caregivers express emotion?
- How did they expect me to express it?
- How did my parents/caregivers respond when I expressed emotion?
- Were certain emotions "unacceptable"?
- Did certain emotions automatically lead to problematic behaviors or actions?
- Was I "allowed" to have my own feelings? Were they valued?

Facing uncomfortable emotions helps you grow—and is ultimately more satisfying in the long run.

Whether it's listening to critical feedback at work, acknowledging your resentment of a loved one, facing your sadness about the loss of a friendship, or any other emotional state you find challenging, the less you avoid it, the stronger you become at navigating those emotions in the future. You give yourself a gift when you let yourself experience it.

Rethink Your Emotions Using These Four Truths

Repairing your relationship with your feelings begins with accepting the following four truths. See if you struggle with any of the following concepts.

1 You have a right to your feelings, any and all of them.

2 Feelings aren't inherently "bad."

3 Having a feeling is not the same as acting destructively on it.

4 Feelings tend to pass if you make space for them and let them breathe, and if you gain insight into what's behind them, rather than running from them.

Take some time to let yourself remember. What comes up? Are there certain feelings you learned to think of as "bad"? Was it "irresponsible" to express certain emotions? Embarrassing? A sign of weakness? Or maybe certain feelings seemed dangerous, because the only way you saw them expressed was in hurting other people. Or your parents always tried so desperately and quickly to soothe your feelings that being upset became taboo, or you were constantly told what or how to feel. ("Come on, you're OK!" "There's no reason to cry!" "That couldn't have hurt!") The more you can pinpoint what dysfunctional stories you have absorbed about emotions, the more prepared you will be to identify those stories as unreliable narrators when they attempt to control your mood.

Making the Case for Feeling Our Feelings

Let's now figure out what stories you tell yourself about your ability to *handle* emotion. As with our thoughts about our thoughts, our feelings about our feelings are almost more important than our feelings themselves. Behind so many anxious thought patterns is what is referred to as mood intolerance or distress intolerance, where we don't believe we can handle difficult, uncomfortable emotions—which increases our avoidance of them even further. If you are prone to this, you may often find yourself thinking things like:

I can't handle this!

•

This is too much for me!

•

I am not strong enough for this!

•

This has got to stop!

•

This is unbearable!

•

I can't cope with this!

•

I am a mess!

•

I am out of control!

•

None of those messages tell us much about the emotion itself. But they all say that you feel you're not capable of handling it, that the feeling is too big for you.

Unfortunately, this thought just makes the feeling seem bigger.

I often have clients who are terrified to "feel" their discomfort. They are scared to talk about something or they'll "never stop crying." They don't want to bring something up because it is "too painful." And yes, it is absolutely true that when someone is in the throes of trauma or intense crisis or loss, *they* should be the ones to guide the pace of what they share. I would never force someone to relive something excruciating—that is re-traumatization, and it's never OK. But when you are in the driver's seat and choose to lean in a bit to your pain and discomfort, you reclaim the energy you had been spending on keeping that emotion at bay. And that emotion starts to become less powerful over you. You are taking control back on your own terms, showing yourself you are capable of moving forward through whatever is happening.

New research shows that people who are able to label their emotions and differentiate them—looking at them with clear, open eyes, rather than trying to run from them—are at lower risk of depression compared with those who have similar negative feelings but don't make a practice of distinguishing them. Acknowledging what you are up against can help you find new ways to cope. If you can make room for your negative feelings as well as your positive ones, owning and accepting their presence in the moment, creating space for them, then you—quite ironically—can help them on their way.

When you feel an uncomfortable emotion, like sadness, guilt, fear, anger, or shame, you may be tempted to take your mind off it right away.

You may have the urge to talk yourself out of it, flee it, or deny it. It feels enticing to put those feelings in a box and stash it all somewhere. But just as stashing your thoughts and pretending they don't exist will backfire, stashing your feelings doesn't work either. That gives them power, and we remain viscerally aware that they are lurking somewhere, so scary that we couldn't even face them, agitating our peripheral nervous system. They're still winning over us.

You Can Handle This:
An Exercise in Physical Discomfort

The stories you tell yourself about your ability to manage physical discomfort may closely parallel your stories about emotional discomfort, or they may not. But since emotions and physical experiences can be closely linked, it's important to observe them both. Are you up for it?

Try not to blink. For as long as possible. It feels surprisingly uncomfortable after only a few seconds, so you might not last very long with this one. Did you observe yourself not blinking? What did you tell or ask yourself—besides *Why is she making me do this*? Did you start to feel panicky? Did you challenge yourself to get to a certain amount of time, or to the end of this paragraph, with the idea that you'd be "failing" if you didn't? Did you immediately give up to find relief, removing yourself from the whole endeavor because it was too hard? Did you find the rest of your body tensing up, and if so, did you address that, or did that just make you more anxious? Did you try desperately to avoid the discomfort and think of something else entirely?

Fill a large mixing bowl (or a small bin) with very cold or even icy water. Commit to keeping your hands in it for thirty seconds and observe yourself tolerating the discomfort. How did you manage it? What did you tell yourself? Did you say you couldn't handle it? Did you assume it would get worse before it got better? Did you trust yourself to get through it, or did you desperately go someplace else in your mind, trying to remove yourself from the experience? What helped and what didn't?

The stories you noticed are important. They are likely the same ones you turn to when experiencing distress in daily life—even when you don't realize you're telling yourself anything at all.

If you want to work further on this, try each exercise again another time (we'll let your hands get back to normal for now). This time, instead of just observing yourself, actively try to open yourself up to the discomfort. Lean into it. Breathe slowly and mindfully and expansively through it. Own it. Feel it. Experience it. Live it. Let it in. You need not ruminate on it, but don't run from it—see if you can find that sweet spot.

Does that change the experience?

Did you surprise yourself, in that it ended up making it a little less uncomfortable?

The research bears this out: Mindfulness interventions increase pain tolerance. By fully facing and acknowledging our experience, we make it less frightening and intense, even though we assume that the opposite would be true.

You *can* handle this. Empower yourself to expand wide enough and open enough to accommodate the discomfort. Sit with it. Make room for it. You are handling it—and getting stronger at moving through it.

What's It Like to Sit with Uncomfortable Emotions?

At first, it can be surprisingly hard.

And that's why we're going to do it.

I want you to sit absolutely still and do nothing, watch nothing, listen to nothing, for *five whole minutes*. For those of you who are used to meditating, try not to launch into anything systematic. I just want you to sit with the nothing.

There's a chance you are making excuses to skip this. Maybe sitting still for five whole minutes with nothing to "occupy" you sounds worse than an appendectomy. Maybe you were about to close the book in two minutes anyway. But please, don't skip it. In fact, if you are desperate to skip it—because the idea of it seems so useless, so frustrating, so "Good grief, are you kidding me?"—then that tells you something important.

What is it about your own mental experience that you want so much to escape?

Some of you might think that this is too easy. You might see the exercise as useless because you think it won't be hard at all. If that turns out to be true, brilliant! But let's try it all the same. Set that timer, and commit to five whole minutes with no phone, podcast, music, book, TV, computer, or any non-digital distraction either.

Get in a comfortable position and just *be*. I'll be here when you get back.

Building Your Mood Tolerance Muscle

So, what did you notice?

Where did your thoughts go? A to-do list? Negative self-talk? Fear? Wondering if you should let yourself cut the exercise short? I gave you no specific instruction about how to handle your thoughts. Perhaps you already started using some of our techniques to handle them peacefully.

But which thoughts and physical sensations came up on their own tells you something. Did you feel antsy? Did you think you were wasting your time? Did you fear you were missing out on something that you could have been scrolling to and discovering? Did you feel lonely and disconnected? Did you make plans for how to reward yourself at the blessed moment that the time was up—perhaps with a deep dive into your phone or a bowl of chips?

In this case, I had forbidden you to use any escape routes, so you really did tolerate the itches—at least for five minutes (if you lasted that long). And congratulations—that gradually builds your mood tolerance muscle! This means it will be a little bit easier next time, and you can become more content *without* your itch-scratchers, because the itches themselves will become less bothersome.

Even if you didn't have any truly difficult thoughts or physical sensations during that little exercise, my guess is that unless you are wonderfully practiced at meditation, you at least felt pretty bored. And in our culture, that feeling can seem pretty excruciating.

In modern life, we have come to view boredom as something to be avoided, but boredom has a brilliant underbelly, a meaningful purpose. It allows for space and light. It gives your mind some room to breathe and meander.

Malcolm in Constant Motion

Thirty-six-year-old Malcolm came to therapy at the behest of his wife and their couples counselor. He was a self-described workaholic, with several dozen employees under his supervision, and his wife felt that he was "quick to yell" and often unduly negative and rigid in parenting their two children. He had identified being more patient as a goal for several years, but she had not seen any difference, and their arguments were frequent. When I listened to a description of Malcolm's daily life, I was struck by how he was always in motion, physically or psychologically—from his early-morning workouts to his frequent work travel, from his long-term plans for his company to his constant making of agendas for the kids' weekend activities. It was clear that he was more than a little antsy about making time for therapy, but as his wife had recently given him an ultimatum, he felt that he had no choice but to put in a few sessions.

When I asked Malcolm to spend the first few minutes of our second therapy session just sitting and *being*, I'm pretty sure he wanted to walk out (or file a malpractice complaint). I caught his eyes making the rounds at not one but two of the clocks I had in the room, in addition to his watch. Twice his arm went to his pocket for his phone, though he resisted the urge to take it out.

When I asked him to reflect on how he had felt, it was very tough for him at first to go deeper than "frustrated," "on edge," and like he was "wasting time." So instead, I asked him to tell me the pros and cons of always being in motion, of having every minute pegged and accounted for, of constantly working toward something, of making sure his kids never had much idle time.

This came more easily to him. Malcolm said he saw his way of life as a very specific answer to a very specific problem: preventing his family from falling into financial instability. It turned out he had grown up with a father who fell in and out of jobs, moving the family often, which even led to living in their car for various periods. Malcolm's mother held various jobs but had only an eighth-grade education. She was severely limited in her ability to find well-paying work while providing the majority of childcare, and she sustained injuries in a car accident when Malcolm was a teenager that further hindered her ability to find a job. All the while, his father belittled his mother and did little to support the family emotionally, and when Malcolm grew taller than him by age fifteen, their arguments grew frequent and physically threatening.

"It was terrifying," Malcolm said.

It was the first feeling he had expressed in almost two hours of working together.

"Was?" I asked. "Or *is?*"

Malcolm looked surprised, as he explained that of course he had risen above that fear, that he was worlds away from following in the path of his parents—he'd gotten not only a college degree but an MBA and was now climbing high on the management ladder. He was able to provide for high-quality care for his mother in an assisted living facility, and his father had passed away fifteen years before. He had left that life and those feelings far behind.

"So, what do you think happened to that fear from all those years? Did that box just get checked off?" I asked.

He thought about this for a moment, and finally acknowledged that he simply didn't let himself feel it.

"And what about the anger?"

He chuckled. "I don't sit around and FEEL anger," he said. "I just do something about whatever's making me angry. Doesn't everyone?"

Finally, we were on to something.

In further work together, it became clear: Malcolm had taught himself over time that *all* fear was to be avoided, rather than experienced, and he attempted this through constant, proactive action. *What if I can't ultimately control how my children's lives turn out?* Then try harder to micromanage their grades. *What if the economy takes a turn and I get laid off?* Then bring more and more work home at night. *What if life is uncertain, and things like a car accident can turn everything upside down in a heartbeat?* Then don't think about it. Just make sure your lives are as planned and predictable as possible to try to stave that off.

His anger, on the other hand, was almost constantly expressed, with the idea that it could be used to make things "right." Teenage Malcolm, for years, was desperate to make his anger *mean* something—to use it to change his father, to scare him into being more of a provider. Malcolm yelled at his dad to try to get him to hear that he needed to treat his mother better. There was nothing worse to Malcolm than lying in bed at night and feeling angry and scared, without immediately doing something about it. That just made him more angry and scared. He always made a plan for the next day; feelings meant nothing unless you did something with them.

As Malcolm went through early adulthood and achieved, achieved, and achieved, gaining more and more power in the process, he convinced himself that he didn't have to make time for feelings: He had conquered them through action.

But life still happened, and anger and fear were still part of it—and always would be, for all of us. And this left Malcolm woefully ill-equipped to manage those emotions more constructively. To him, fear meant "go faster and work harder." And anger meant "overpower whoever's causing the problem." Both of which led to overwork, impatience, rigidity, an inability to enjoy the moment, and much barking at his loved ones—which was ruining his marriage.

Experiencing a Feeling
Is Not the Same as Acting on It

Malcolm tended to act automatically on his emotions. For other people, it's the *fear* of acting automatically on emotions that makes them want to avoid them; they think there is no experiencing an emotion without acting on it. Are you having trouble granting yourself the right to truly experience your feelings? Let's try a reframe.

Let's say Megan slipped down the stairs at the house of her friend Keisha and broke her leg. Megan really liked Keisha as a person; they were close. So, should Megan try to convince herself that she shouldn't get medical treatment for her leg, that the pain wasn't real, just because she liked Keisha so much? Should Megan tell herself it's not "fair" for her to have a broken leg, since Keisha never meant for the stairs to hurt her and feels terrible about it? Megan didn't want Keisha to feel worse. So should Megan walk around on the broken leg for the foreseeable future, because she "shouldn't" have a broken leg since Keisha never intended for that to happen? Or suppose Megan's bones were particularly weak due to a condition she's always had. Would she still deserve to seek medical attention for her leg?

Of course she would. Her leg needed treatment. Fairness isn't part of the equation, even if Megan were particularly prone to broken legs, and even though Keisha never meant for her to get hurt. *Megan's leg is broken.*

Sometimes it's your feelings that need treatment—or at least acknowledgment. If someone you love makes you angry, the question of whether it's "fair" to have that anger is really beside the point. You have the feeling. It's there. And if you stuff it or ignore it or try to talk yourself out of it, it will only corrode things further. We wouldn't ignore the broken leg, but we try to ignore feelings all the time. We believe so wholeheartedly that we should be able to control them and make them disappear, and we even wonder whether we "deserve" to feel them in the first place.

For those of you cringing at the idea of letting yourself feel all your feelings, take note: *Acknowledging a feeling need not mean acting on it.* Being angry with a loved one is different than directing that anger toward them in a negative way, for instance. Maybe sometimes you'll choose not to bring up your anger or disappointment to your loved one because you know they are stressed or preoccupied, or you just want to give them a pass. That's OK. But that shouldn't mean internally denying your feelings.

And maybe, with the broken leg example, Megan won't scream at Keisha, or take a blowtorch to her stairs, or sue her. But she will acknowledge that her leg is broken. It's the same with feelings: Acknowledging them does not necessarily mean acting on them. That's an entirely different calculation. As with anger, *feeling angry at someone is not the same thing as harming them.*

Emotions Pass, Too

In ACT, one analogy for emotions is that they are the weather of your mind. They change; they intensify; they come and they go. And yet there is always weather, just like you always feel something—even if it feels like you're feeling the *absence* of something. Anhedonia—the loss of pleasure and interest that often occurs in depression—is sometimes seen as the lack of feeling something. But looked at a different way, it can also be seen as an active, present weather pattern—like cloudiness being the absence of sunshine. There can be different levels of cloudiness, and different levels of emotional numbness.

If you work toward being able to tolerate negative emotions as you would the weather, you are better able to prepare yourself for them, and to remind yourself that they will pass. You may know that meeting with your boss could make you angry. Or that the anniversary of your mother's death will make you sad. Or that attempting to initiate a mortgage loan will make you anxious. These feelings are all OK. And the more you anticipate them and make room for them, the stronger and better prepared you will be in passing through them (or letting them pass through you).

Sitting with a Feeling

How do you really own a feeling? How do you make yourself open to it, and sit with it—and not succumb to the temptation to talk yourself out of it, mask it, distract yourself from it, or avoid it?

Like many things in this book, it takes practice.

The first step is to ground yourself in the moment. If your thoughts are spiraling too far into the future (like wanting to act on the emotion) or rewinding too far into the past (like ruminating on why something had to happen to cause this emotion in the first place), gently reconnect yourself to the here and now.

Return to Get Grounded on page 59, and pay special attention to how the emotion feels in your body.

Notice the thoughts you are having about the emotion.

This will break me!

●

What if this never stops?

●

I hate this!

●

Gently recognize those thoughts as fleeting words, labeling them and acknowledging that they are not helpful or accurate.

No, this emotion won't break you. It would be there in some form whether you stuffed it or not, and it will pass more quickly if you acknowledge it.

Yes, it will stop. Feelings fade and change like the weather.

Yes, you hate this. If some of your mental statements are true, you can still reframe them to be more helpful. What's also true about you hating this is that you are learning to tolerate something that really, really bothers you, and that is important. Your hatred of this shows just how much strength you are building, and what the payoff can be. So there's quite a beneficial underlayer in *I hate this.*

Now, go back to the negative emotion and imagine it in a visual way—texture, size, color, and temperature—and visualize how, at least for this very moment, you are able to open yourself up to be big enough for it. You are here, with this feeling, just where you are supposed to be.

I've worked with many people suffering from grief and loss, and two feelings that I often hear are "This is too much for me" or "This won't ever get better. The grief will never let up." (And their friends may feel uncomfortable with this, not knowing what to say, wanting to help the feeling go faster to the point where they have "moved on.")

But one conceptualization that some of my clients have responded well to, while we sit with their feelings of grief together, is this: Yes, this loss will remain with you. It will always be there, and it may not get smaller. *But you will get bigger around it.* It will eventually cease feeling like too much for you to carry, even as you continue to carry it. Waves of grief will come and go, and some of them will be intense and feel harder than the day before. But you will continue growing. Grief expert David Kessler puts the goal of that growth this way: In time, you'll remember the person you lost with more love than pain.

The same principle applies to pretty much any feeling—from nervousness to anger, from irritation to shame (as long as it isn't so traumatizing and paralyzing that it needs a bit more intensive help). You will grow bigger. But you have to open yourself up to that growth first. Are you willing to do that? Are you willing to trust yourself and your strength? Are you willing to put this into practice—to lean into your feelings, own them, and know that ultimately, no weather pattern stays exactly the same forever?

Malcolm, Learning from Stillness

To Malcolm's credit, he was. It took time, certainly, but Malcolm began to practice acknowledging his emotions—fear and anger in particular—without automatically speeding toward distracting himself from them or acting on them. He learned to recognize his feelings in the moment and understand how they affected his bodily responses. ("I'm worried because I didn't get as far on that report as I had planned before leaving work. It's making my muscles tense and I feel on edge, like I'm unprepared and going to be 'caught.'") In time, he was better able to counteract these bodily responses—("I'll do some stretches that target my neck, and do five minutes with some free weights while going big on inhales and exhales")—which made him less jittery, impatient, and agitated.

Giving his feelings labels also allowed him to communicate them to others—his wife in particular—which helped her feel connected to him and like they could work out problems together as a team. When they would argue, he found it much easier to wait a moment, collect his thoughts about what he was experiencing, and express it in the form of the "I" statements that their couples counselor had long been urging but he had always been unable to put into practice. ("I'm feeling annoyed that the kids weren't ready to go as planned when I came home to get them for the banquet. Being late is stressful for me, and I think it's important they make a good impression. I feel like we're not on the same page about this stuff sometimes, which makes me anxious.") He adjusted his big picture to include the fact that he couldn't absolutely guarantee how his children would turn out, but that he could do his best to raise them with the values he and his wife believed in. And that the uncertainty was part of life, and it was something he could sit with—no frantic micromanaging weekends needed.

Malcolm was never meant to become some uber-serene guy meditating on a mountaintop, and that was totally OK. On the surface, he was still an ambitious, energized person with high standards for his employees and his family. But when he committed to spend time each day sitting with his feelings—a ten-minute "mental break" ritual helped immensely—he learned how to move toward the things in life he truly wanted most, rather than being in constant motion just for the *sake* of movement.

A Feeling as a Guidepost

It's also important to give some thought to what your difficult feeling is trying to tell you. If you pretended this feeling was a teacher, what would its lesson be? If you gave this feeling the benefit of the doubt and assumed it was there for a purpose, what would that purpose look like?

These answers often guide you toward actions that are healthier and more helpful than your automatic urges. Feelings can spur you to solve an ongoing problem (like planning a thoughtful, respectful discussion with a loved one about something bothering you, rather than just snapping at them or giving them the silent treatment). Or you may be driven toward action to honor the feeling, like channeling your anger at injustice into working for social change, or deciding to reach out and connect with those going through the same challenges that you are.

But other times, there is no action needed beyond feeling the feeling itself, and giving yourself permission to be fully in it without running from it.

So many of us have real difficulty with that. Keep trying.

Surfing Your Urges

Sometimes the urge to escape an uncomfortable emotion is so strong that it uses all its might to direct you toward one specific behavior: I'm talking about cravings. If you are in recovery from substance abuse addiction, or are trying to curtail binge-eating, smoking, self-harm, chewing your nails, or a porn habit, your body and mind may together conspire to turn all your focus to how desperate you are to engage in that behavior.

But a craving, no matter how strong or biologically driven, can be ridden out the same way an uncomfortable emotion can: It will pass. Many people believe that they must go to war with their cravings in order not to give in; they confuse rising above an urge with fighting it. But remember, fighting an urge only gives it more attention and power. Your goal should not be to talk yourself out of it. A much better practice is to label a craving and observe it, as if it were a passing wave that you will ride. This is "urge-surfing," a technique originated by the late addiction treatment pioneer Alan Marlatt. It goes like this:

1. Acknowledge the craving.
2. Feel it in your body, and be a gentle, nonjudgmental observer of it.
3. Let it pass through you, which it will do, even if it eventually comes back again (and when it does, you can employ the same techniques).

In time, the waves will lose their power to threaten you—because you have learned to ride them without being knocked over.

My clients with bulimia or binge-eating issues in particular are typically quite resistant to the idea that their urge to binge will ever pass on its own. And it's true that sitting with that urge feels very, very tough at first. But I have them do a little experiment: I ask them to postpone a binge for a half hour after they initially feel the urge. Usually, they'll immediately ask: "What's the point, if I'm going to binge anyway?" I ask them just to try, and to notice and sit with their craving in the meantime, along with identifying any of the physical and emotional feelings that are driving it. When they actually commit to doing it, you can probably guess the outcome: Not only do they learn how to better understand and manage their urges, increasing their coping ability for difficult feelings, but—just by giving it a half hour—the craving often passes, so they end up no longer binge-ing at all.

Leaning into your feelings without distraction

Discomfort is not the enemy; it is an inevitable part of life. When you learn to let it pass through you with less fear, then you can move forward without it defining you.

1 **ACKNOWLEDGE** your automatic distractors of choice. It may take a day or two of observing yourself, and it may be embarrassing. I'm not asking you to change anything yet; I want you just to observe. How many times did you unlock your smartphone when you weren't really planning to, just reaching for it to scratch an itch? Maybe it's food, vaping, or wine. Maybe it's biting your nails until they bleed, excessively watching porn, or driving yourself into debt with online purchases. Maybe it's any number of other things.

2 **STOP** yourself in the middle of running toward your distractors, in the moment. Slow yourself down and just be. Take a breath and observe yourself. Notice any physical sensations, thoughts, and emotions. Ask yourself: *What am I running from, and what might happen if I just sat with this instead? Is there a path* through *this feeling that's better for me?*

3 **ADJUST** your mind-set to make room for discomfort. Does it have to be viewed as a bad thing? Are there ways it can contribute toward insight or growth? Consider, too, the way you think about boredom. Can you build in times in your day or week that are more open, allowing your mind some additional space?

PART III

Your Heart

> *"Someone I loved once gave me a box full of darkness. It took me years to understand that this, too, was a gift."*
>
> **MARY OLIVER**

6

You Chase Pleasure and Miss Out on Meaning

WHAT DOES IT MEAN TO BE "HAPPY," ANYWAY?

So many of us say that's what we want. If we have kids, it's on the greatest hits list of what we say we want for our children. And yet, it can be defined in so many different ways. Let's talk first about two different conceptualizations of happiness. While there is overlap between the two, they sometimes get in each other's way.

HEDONIC HAPPINESS involves joy, pleasure, and just feeling *good*. Pain and discomfort are reduced, the brain is at ease, and you feel pretty content. (*This brownie tastes delicious!*)

EUDAIMONIC HAPPINESS is less easily summed up with a dessert analogy. This experience does not require complete comfort or satisfaction, nor does it necessarily entail the heights of pleasure. Instead, it means that you are in touch with your purpose in life, and are engaged in growth and discovery. You are living in accordance with your values, even when it is challenging. Eudaimonic happiness involves a sense of autonomy, but also the feeling of belonging and connection to something greater than yourself.

In the pursuit of happiness, we need a mix of both hedonic and eudaimonic experiences in life. Nonetheless, the research on long-term well-being strongly suggests that if we consistently search for happiness purely in the pleasure realm, we will—quite ironically—end up not very happy at all.

Think of the celebrity whose mental health flames out after a whirlwind of mansions, lovers, and private jets. The narrative is familiar. After a while, a feeling of emptiness and disconnection crept in. The superstar—though they were able to indulge every whim—lost their sense of human connection, their reason for being, and their opportunity to find new depths in themselves.

Their "pleasure" was so consistently devoid of meaning that it started to look an awful lot like numbness.

People in such situations grow to miss the satisfaction of working for something, the challenge and sense of purpose it brings. It becomes harder to align daily actions with deeper values. Retirement can be a difficult transition for the same reason. (Chapter 10 continues this analysis with a discussion of the myth of arrival. If someone assumes that retirement or striking it rich is key to their happiness, they're in for disappointment.)

Hedonic happiness satiates your senses with pleasures that can feel very, very good in the moment. But that doesn't necessarily connect you with deeper meaning. Because finding meaning involves challenging yourself—and growing along the way. Deeper meaning often involves struggle, yet it's what brings us the most profound satisfaction and fulfillment in the long run.

Have you ever watched a time-lapse video of a seed coming out of its pod and growing into a full-fledged plant, from underground speck to full bloom? I highly recommend it, even if your interest in gardening is limited to the fake succulents on your office desk.

It looks almost violent, that struggle. The little seedling bursts out above the dirt, and now it is terrifyingly exposed—to wind, chill, and rain. It is completely vulnerable to whatever may come to meet it, like my clumsy watering techniques or my overly inquisitive dog. No doubt the seed would have been more comfortable in the short term if it remained snug in the dirt, safe from all threat. That seems infinitely more calming than tearing itself open to the world.

And yet it's opening itself to the world, with all the risk that entails, that allows it to blossom.

The truth is both simple and scary: The seed must take a risk in order to grow and be fully *alive*. And though it is not comfortable, it's the only way it will ever see the sun. There's no other method for development and growth. There's no other way to eventually experience the larger world—connecting to a universe that is fuller and more complex than the tiny dark hole where it started.

In this sense, we humans aren't much different. Growth takes vulnerability, and it often strips us of our comfort. A bajillion motivational personalities have already noted this: To improve ourselves, we must step out of our comfort zones. But they often leave out what this truly means in terms of pleasure.

The truth is, we probably must give up a bit of hedonic happiness to increase our chances at eudaimonic happiness in the long term. This sounds frightening, sacrificing comfort for a more meaningful sense of fulfillment. We may sometimes even have to miss a little momentary pleasure in order to open ourselves more deeply and fully to our lives.

A long-ago client of mine, Amir, who was not a native English speaker, used to refer to this process as "engaging with the fabric of life." He was prone to anxiety and depression, but to him, the measure of how he was doing was not smiley faces or fleeting joys (though those were certainly nice). The meaningful stuff was more subtle than that, but much, much deeper. It was being truly present—and fully alive. It was choosing to live wholly, and experience all that life entailed, making room for every bit of it. *The opposite of his depression wasn't pleasure.* It was being fully here, open-eyed and open-armed to what life would bring to him, even when that was sometimes difficult. *Engaging with the fabric of life.*

I thought that was beautiful.

People who have found and embraced sobriety after years of attempting to numb or dull their painful feelings with substances will often speak of a similar mind-set shift. They have learned to live in a different way than before. This new way of living is not automatically more pleasurable, but it is more authentic and ultimately more fulfilling. They have learned to prioritize feeling things—all of it, highs and lows both—over hiding or getting a momentary jolt of escape. They are ready to open themselves up to life.

They are ready to engage.

Ask Yourself These Tough but Important Questions

One of the surest ways to prioritize eudaimonic happiness is living out what you feel to be your sense of purpose. It is, of course, living your "best life"—but in the age of Instagram, it's easy to forget that what defines this goes far deeper than having a lifestyle that can be captured for others in the perfect snapshot. A sense of purpose isn't something you can see visually—and though seeking beauty may be part of it for you, it's an internal feeling, not an external setting.

Trying to figure out your life's purpose may be stressful in and of itself. That's OK. You don't have to have the answers right now, nor do you have to sign on some "Here's My Life's Purpose!" dotted line and keep that focus forevermore.

But you do need to be willing to ask yourself questions as you go along. Open yourself to the observation of what activities, experiences, goals, and relationships resonate most deeply with you, even if they're not what you would have expected. Ask yourself if your go-to activities truly connect you with something bigger than temporary sensations of pleasure or comfort.

If you feel like you don't have any idea of what can bring you a sense of meaning or purpose, take heart: That can be good. It means you're not wedded to a preconceived notion of what your life "should" be about, and that you can open yourself to discovering it—if you are willing. Here are some questions to guide your thinking, and remember: Answering them is a process, not a one-time event.

WHAT WOULD YOU DO WITH
A TOTALLY FREE DAY?

How would you spend a completely open day with no responsibilities whatsoever? Imagine also that you are fully rested and recharged, so you need not spend the day napping or taking a mental health break—you're ready to put your energies and talents to use. To what, or to whom, would you devote your time?

If you chose something that feels like a pleasurable time-filler with no greater sense of meaning, that's OK. But try now to go a little deeper. Imagine instead that you had not just one day to fill, but a week, a month, or even a year. Presumably, that Netflix binge would get old after a while. (And if not? Perhaps you should be pursuing a side gig as a TV critic.)

HOW WOULD YOU WANT YOUR
LIFE TO BE SUMMED UP SOMEDAY?

What would you want included in your obituary? How would you like to be described? Think about the legacy you want to leave. Everyone changes the world in their own way by having been here. The "small" acts matter immensely too. What is it that you want to have done, not just accomplishments that could be listed on a résumé, but rather in the ripple effects of small daily actions? What energy do you want to pass on to others?

This certainly doesn't mean that you must have the arc of your professional or social life figured out. You may end up with a career you have no idea of yet, a partner you have yet to meet (or a single life that surprises you with how fulfilling it is). But you can start thinking about what feels worth your time now.

WHAT ARE YOU THE MOST WILLING
TO PUT EFFORT INTO?

What you choose to spend energy on offers a glimpse into what carries deeper value for you. Such activities may not even feel much like work. Of course, people who claim to love their jobs one hundred percent of the time naturally raise our suspicions. And it's neither realistic nor helpful to expect that anything—even something or someone you're passionate about—should bring you nonstop joy. (That would be falling into the trap of valuing hedonic happiness over its eudaimonic counterpart.) But your energy is finite—and when you find yourself choosing to spend it on certain things, that gives you a clue as to your priorities.

WHOSE FACES DO YOU SEE WHEN
YOU HEAR THE WORD "LOVE"?

A meaningful part of my own career involves speaking to audiences about the sense of meaning that relationships can bring. For many of us, a significant part of our life's purpose involves connecting with others. It's beautiful and quantifiable at the same time: As we'll discuss in Chapter 8, having quality social connections is one of the most significant predictors of mental and physical health, including longevity.

And relationships can be the heart and soul of what makes life worth living. Caregiving—not just for children, but for parents, friends, pets, partners, neighbors, or other loved ones—is one of the clearest examples of an activity that doesn't always bring pleasure but can most definitely be associated with a deeper level of meaning and fulfillment over time.

WHAT ACTIVITIES PUT YOU IN FLOW?

"Flow"—a concept coined by Mihaly Csikszentmihalyi—happens when you are engaged in an experience with the ideal blend of interest and challenge, so you are neither bored nor stressed nor numb. You may lose your sense of time, feeling positively immersed in an experience for its own sake.

Even if you hate your job overall, maybe you're in flow for parts of it, feeling more alive in those moments. Interacting with the public? Brainstorming a project? Researching? Creating something? Supporting others? Following through on details? Sharing an idea? Completing a job? Satisfying a customer? Making a difference?

If you've never experienced flow, don't despair. You just need more exploration, and a willingness to challenge the assumptions you've been holding. It could be worth consulting a career counselor to take assessments of your interests, personality traits, strengths, and challenges, to help identify potentially fulfilling paths for you.

Values That Guide Your Purpose

Of course not every day will feel fully aligned with your sense of purpose, and that's completely fine. But that's where values come in. The more you know what feels meaningful and purposeful to you, the better you can establish values in accordance with that sense of purpose. Values help steer your life, even on those days when you need a pretty heavy hit of hedonic experiences that have nothing to do with your sense of purpose. Values help show you the way to stay true to your sense of purpose.

They help you feel truer to yourself as you go through life, even on your off days. They mesh well with your sense of purpose and reflect it, just as your sense of purpose likely reflects those values as well.

Arriving at these values isn't meant to be the end goal. Instead, these values are ways to live along the way. And it's not about choosing values as a means to an end that is admired by others. It's about letting your values guide and sustain you in the little moments: the ambiguous, boring, or painful times, and the confusing ones where you are unsure which direction to take.

What are *your* values?

Think of them as the ways that you choose to interact with the world. What guiding ideals do you believe in?

- ☐ Integrity?

- ☐ Compassion?

- ☐ Humor?

- ☐ Freedom?

- ☐ Intellectual engagement?

- ☐ Helping others?

- ☐ Being an individual?

- ☐ Energy and movement?

- ☐ Being part of a community?

- ☐ Justice?

- ☐ Curiosity?

- ☐ Artistic expression?

- ☐ Adventure?

- ☐ Peace?

- ☐ Independence?

- ☐ Challenging the status quo?

- ☐ Something else?

Next, think about all the ways you can live out these values in moments big and small throughout your life, at home and at work, alone and with others. Remember: These values are not the end picture of who you are supposed to "be," or where you are supposed to end up. They are the guiding forces that help you along the way. Values exist for their own sake; they are how you choose to live. They're not ways of being that you expect to yield a certain reward in return.

The reward is the living itself.

Dave and the Pain of the Misstep

What about the mistakes we make along the way? Even living according to our values can sometimes lead us astray when we make choices that cause us harm. Feeling like we screwed up, or falling short of a vision we had for ourselves, can be excruciating, and our brain itches for a "delete" key for our mistake. This is why near misses are usually more painful than being off by a mile: We allowed ourselves to envision a prized outcome, and it slipped away. What we fell short of—whether a jackpot on a game show or a long-term commitment with the one who got away—felt almost real, and then it was gone. The experience feels more akin to *losing* something than to having never won it in the first place.

With regrets, we ruminate on why we didn't do things differently at that one particular point—a similar dynamic. The "prize" we lost was the ability to take a different path, and our brain is desperate for that "undo" option. We tend to see a mistake as an individual entity, as if it were a singular action with an on-off switch, rather than one point in the interconnected continuum of our lives.

But any one event on your life's path is inextricably tied to all the others. Not only can it not be undone, but it is part of what led to your here and now. What if it feels like your mistake taught you nothing? Then you might need a new way to look at that regret. My client Dave and I found one.

Dave was a thirty-four-year-old father of two who just could not shake a certain "if only": having invested nearly all of his savings in a friend's restaurant that went belly-up. In Dave's estimation, there was nothing he learned from it (besides a wholly unsatisfying "Don't do that again"), and he certainly didn't believe it made him stronger. Dave often played out in his mind what his life would have looked like had he not invested: how much more money and less stress he would have, how his wife wouldn't have to work in the job she hated. He viewed the investment choice as a switch that he flipped, and felt that his life could be redeemed if only he could find a way to undo the switch. This weighed on his mind from morning until night and debilitated him.

Finding Meaning in Regrets

What is the story you tell yourself about your missteps in life? It's important to remember that taking risks is part of growth, and risk-taking involves mistake-making. It's hard to imagine doing anything creative, or truly growing or progressing, while somehow living a life completely devoid of mistakes. Of course, some risks are just not wise, even if they'll skyrocket your You-Tube subscribers—I'm certainly not advising you to embrace recklessness or to avoid thinking carefully about your choices. But once a mistake has been made, it's a sunk cost, as you've learned. Remember, the best way to recoup that "investment" is to find some meaning in it and figure out what it can teach you.

When you ruminate on a regret, it means it's embedded itself, like the most negative of automatic thoughts. Such regrets force your attention onto themselves as if they have something important to say, changing your mood for the worse. And you may keep reexperiencing the regrets as if you are back in the moment, as with trauma. So the negative emotional response can become chronic over time. In my practice, I've seen regrets lead to patterns of these recurring emotions:

- **HUMILIATION:** *I can't believe I did that. I bet they'll never look at me the same way again. How can I ever show my face?*
- **SHAME:** *Everyone must think I'm a bad person now. I probably am—why else would I have done that?*
- **GUILT:** *I'll never be able to take this back. I did damage, and it's unforgivable.*
- **SADNESS:** *If only I hadn't done that, so much would have turned out differently. Nothing will ever be the same now.*
- **ANGER:** *What an absolute idiot I am to have done that. I don't even deserve to be happy.*
- **FEAR:** *Clearly I can't even trust myself to do the right thing. What if I screw up again?*
- **HELPLESSNESS:** *I'll never be able to get over this.*
- **HOPELESSNESS:** *I don't know how I'll ever be able to live with myself.*

The more long-lasting or repetitive these emotional states, the more they affect your beliefs about yourself. That's quite a lot of toxicity for a single mistake, accident, or oversight to bring. Maybe even just a ten-second decision or action, weighing you down for years to come. How hard it can be to let yourself off the hook!

But that's where meaning comes in. If you choose to find meaning in your mistakes, then *you* get to decide what story your mistake tells you and what value it has. And if your regrets are going to be shouting at you anyway, why not provide them with a more functional script?

To start this process, first find your resistance to letting go. What's the barrier? Maybe you feel you've done something so bad that you *deserve* to carry the mental burden of it throughout your life. If that's the case, then you need to work on the process of forgiving yourself (Chapter 7).

Maybe your resistance comes from a place of feeling judged by others. Embarrassment, shame, and humiliation are fierce forces to reckon with, long past the seventh-grade lunchroom. But by holding on to the thoughts that perpetuate these emotions, and continuing to carry the toxic weight of your regret, how are you helping anything? How is other people's judgment—or even worse, what you *fear* of other people's judgment—a valid guide-post to what your own emotional experience should be? Often, our shame about how others see our mistakes prohibits us from taking new risks and growing from them—activities that, ironically, could help repair whatever relationships we feel we fractured in the first place.

Taking the Long View

In my very first session with Dave, he referred to the "toll" the mistake of investing in his friend's business took. So I asked him, "Are there any other tolls you've had to pay in life?"

"Sure," he responded. "I've got a bum knee from an old soccer injury that keeps me more inactive than I'd like." I acknowledged this and asked him for others. "I've got a severe peanut allergy, which always cramps my style in restaurants." He thought some more. "My mother has dementia, which is sometimes hard to cope with."

"And yet you do cope," I pressed.

"Well, yeah, those things just happened," he said. "They can't be helped."

Ah. But wasn't it interesting that his brain wasn't obsessively searching for an undo switch for *those* things? That he wasn't spending his days beating himself up about his soccer injury, obsessing about whether his nut allergy may have been made worse by some early experience, or how he should have found some way to ward off his mother's dementia? He had instead come to a place of acceptance with these things, and had learned to work within them, rather than struggling against them. Why?

"Well, isn't it obvious?" he said. "Because I didn't directly choose any of those."

Interesting. That mind-set revealed more than he realized.

"Choose" was key. Indeed, he had chosen to assume the risk of investing the money. But hadn't he also chosen the risk of playing on the soccer field the day he got injured?

The soccer injury versus investment loss felt like night and day to him in their differences, but I suggested that they were more similar than he realized. He hadn't chosen to lose all his investment, just as he hadn't chosen to get hurt on the soccer field. He had chosen the *path* of the investment, for sure. And that involved assessing risk and agreeing to it. But he had done that exact same thing by choosing to play soccer. And in neither case would continuing to blame himself be helpful or functional. He had made both choices—the soccer and the investment—because he valued doing active things that gave him a sense of movement, adventure, and connection to others.

If getting injured was an acceptable "toll" for the fun of playing soccer, could he also start to view the lost investment as another toll along the path of an exciting, active life? Could that allow him to let go of searching for a way to bargain himself out of his past?

What if we envisioned that lost money not as a mistake to be regretted, but as a toll to willingly pay to choose an adventurous highway in life, to be autonomous and not unduly weighed down by fear?

In time, this new conceptualization helped immensely. Dave reframed his regret with a new story to tell himself: Four years prior, he had been traveling on a path. It was an exciting, daring path, and he enjoyed it and was able to chart his own course, with all the autonomy and responsibility and navigation decisions that entailed. He had seen a new turn on that path—a road that looked particularly interesting as an opportunity—and he chose to take it. When he got near the toll booth, he saw that the toll was particularly expensive. But he had to pay it to continue moving forward, and if he backed off he'd always have wondered what he missed out on. Indeed, he learned things on that path that would make him better suited in his future navigation. And someday, at the end of his life, he would view that payment simply as the price of admission for the privilege of exploring that particular path, a path that led to all others.

Dave had accumulated other tolls too, just as we all do, in the course of our lives' travels. But once we've gone through the toll booth, we're on that path. If we want to keep moving and continue to find new paths, we can't take a U-turn after the fact, wasting our time arguing for a refund that will never come. That squanders time and opportunity. *We've already paid to be on the road.* So let's choose to really live that choice: to look around, see the scenery, and continue the adventure.

I want to get my money's worth, and Dave decided he did as well.

Don't you?

Choosing Your View During the Ride

Think of a regret—an "if only"—that eats away at you. What meaning can you derive from that regret? Here are some questions to get you there.

- Do I know something I didn't before?
- Did I discover new resilience in myself?
- Am I better positioned to make more informed choices in the future?
- Have I discovered a better understanding of what's important in my life and what is not?
- Have I developed closer ties with others?
- Have I seen new depths in myself, my heart, or my mind?
- Have I become more empathetic about other people's struggles?
- Have I learned how to better avoid certain missteps?

Connecting to your sense of purpose

Each day brings small opportunities to live out your values. Feeling that your life is in sync with them helps connect you to a deeper sense of meaning and fulfillment.

1 **THINK** about your own definitions of "happiness," big and small, and what moments tend to bring it. What is the big picture of what it looks like to you? Are there differences between your hedonic moments and your sense of what brings you a more eudaimonic fulfillment over time?

2 **DESCRIBE** your values and your sense of purpose. What words would you use? These may be well fleshed out, or they may be just a start. Begin a mental sketch of what these concepts look like to you, and list activities and experiences—big and small, ambitious and mundane—that can help you connect with these ideas.

3 **REFRAME** a certain challenge or regret in your life as a way to lend depth to your sense of meaning. How can you begin to envision this seemingly negative part of your life as part of a larger picture that is richer because of it? Think of something you have wished to undo or take back, and take a moment to visualize it as something that brought you to the path you are currently on: a path that is full of possibility, and yours for the choosing. Got it? Now try it with another regret.

7

You Seek Approval Over Connection

SO DEVELOPING A SENSE OF PURPOSE and meaning can help you find your sense of worth.

But there are so many things vying to take that sense of worth away. Over the course of your life, you have internalized many different expectations and standards, innumerable "shoulds" and comparisons that form the basis for how you think and feel about yourself. Sadly, they are often fundamentally dysfunctional.

Let's start with something so common that it's probably in your hands far more hours than you want to admit, constantly by your side during the day, and even in your bed at night. Though not everyone is on social media (and if you're not, there's still plenty for you in this chapter), it is the perfect place to begin a discussion about the differences between approval versus true connection and self-worth. (*Here she goes*, you might be saying. *She mentioned smartphones before, but now she's REALLY going to rail against them and social media, and tell me to go live in a yurt after I've given up my phone and completed my acai berry cleanse. I've heard this all before.*)

The backlash against technological advances has followed every major step forward (including the old-school telephone and the telegram). But when, say, Samuel Morse invented the telegraph, he did not pay a cadre of behavioral neuroscience experts to make consumers more addicted to it so that they'd spend more time and more money on it. There's an entire industry whose sole goal is to rewire our brains for its profit. Clearly technology is here to stay, and it's advancing at an exponentially rapid pace. Let's look beyond the black and white and dig into the gray, such as what's better for us online versus what's worse, how we are most susceptible to digital life's dangers, and how we can maximize its benefits. You can get your digital habits to work *for* your mental and emotional health, rather than against them.

How often have you had this experience: You post a selfie on your social media of choice, and it's a nice pic. (You got it on the fourth try!) You liked your smile in it, and your upper arm wasn't doing that thing where it looks like a pork loin. You were at an interesting event that was the perfect sweet spot between "I'm bragging that I got these tickets" and "I'm really, really, REALLY bragging that I got these tickets."

And then . . . things are slow in the response department. You're not seeing much action on your post. (*Are people asleep?* you wonder. *Are they all at some better event without me? Maybe my followers have all been in some kind of terrible accident. Hmm. Well, on the bright side, that would mean they're not ignoring me.*)

Finally, the likes start to pick up. *My husband's old boss liked the post!* There is relief. Maybe a little more relief than you want to admit. *My coworker's essential oils consultant liked it!* You're feeling better. Until you start wondering why your college roommate, your sister, or the-dude-that-likes-almost-everything-and-you-don't-even-remember-how-you-know-him hasn't liked it yet.

This is a common dynamic—so common that it feels like the new normal. Every time you post something, you're putting yourself out there and waiting. You click away; you click back. You refresh. And in the meantime, you're putting your feelings, and maybe even your self-worth, at the mercy of algorithms and Wi-Fi connections. You've added a wall between you and another human, and given it the power to screw with your emotions. For a bit of time—before that first "like" comes, or before you think *enough* likes come (or even after the likes come, if they're not the *right* likes), you've made yourself lonelier. All in order to try to connect and not feel lonely!

Social media has given us a rather strange power: the ability to narrate even the most mundane details of our lives, in real time, to a large and willing audience. (It's hard to imagine how this would have seemed to humans of earlier generations. You may have already heard this from an older relative: "Why would anyone want to see a picture of your soup?") But with that power comes an even greater vulnerability: the constant expectation and need for positive feedback on our choices, our experiences, and even our looks. It's a peculiar time in the history of human relationships. We never had these types of interactions before, and now we have them constantly.

Can you imagine if this cycle of *Did I say it the right way? Do they like me? Was I interesting enough?* happened in person, in real time? You'd be having coffee with a friend, make some triumphant declaration ("I just rocked a job interview!"), and then be waiting there awkwardly and blankly, not knowing if they're even going to respond? Can you imagine being desperate for that friend to give you feedback but not being sure if it would come? It sounds exhausting, like no interactions with friends you'd want to have.

And yet we do the equivalent of this day in and day out online.

But here's the thing: For people with social anxiety disorder, this happens in person too. If you have significant social anxiety, you may have even recognized yourself in that coffee conversation example above. Maybe it didn't sound so unusual after all.

That thought process—*Do they like me? How are they going to respond? Was I interesting enough?*—is called excessive self-monitoring, and it's what we tend to do when we become overly concerned with curating our lives for consumption on social media. And as much as "self-monitoring" sounds like it could be part of the "observe your thoughts" mantra I've been extolling since page 1 of this book, the opposite is true, since it's excessive. Excessive self-monitoring comes with a cruel, judgmental eye. It entails being so hyperalert to everything you say and do that you become your own worst critic—and enemy. It is the opposite of being a gentle, nonjudgmental observer, and it doesn't open your mind, but rather digs you deeper into doubt and anxiety about yourself.

Could it be that part of why social media (in many measures) is associated with increased distress and loneliness is because it's doing just that? Giving all of us an increased sense of social anxiety? A growing and harsh self-judgment, made worse and worse by excessive self-monitoring (which becomes par for the course when we're constantly trying to figure out what our audience wants)? I really think so. I believe we're not just getting more impatient for likes, but in the process, we're getting more anxious and afraid in general.

After all, in twenty years as a therapist, I got pretty used to seeing the obsession of *Do people like me enough?* because I had many clients with social anxiety disorder.

Now, it seems, the *Do people like me enough?* obsession is everywhere.

Loneliness Is a Public Health Problem

Loneliness is not just a terrible feeling, but it can be truly harmful to your health. Data show that feeling chronically lonely and socially unsupported is the equivalent, mortality-wise, of smoking fifteen cigarettes per day. Fifteen cigarettes—that's not a typo. Loneliness makes your prognosis worse for chronic illness, weakens your immune system, and is measurably bad for your heart. Loneliness and the breakdown of communities are increasingly thought to be directly connected to the epidemic of opioid addiction and overdose deaths. In one of the longest-running psychological studies of all time, the Harvard Grant study run by George Vaillant, the quality of interpersonal relationships proved to be among the most salient of factors in *how long people lived*. Plus, for most of us, other people provide depth, a sense of meaning, and fulfillment to our lives as well.

But loneliness is growing more prevalent across the globe, to the point of being labeled a public health crisis. (Great Britain has appointed a minister for loneliness.) And there are various sociological shifts, even independent of technology, that are likely contributing. People now have smaller extended family networks—the number of "kinless" people has gone up significantly—and longer work hours have led to less participation in community and civic activities. Neighbors are less likely to know one another and interact than they did in the past.

The opposite of loneliness is true connection and emotional intimacy. But in the age of social media, true connection—and even friendship—get confusing. On the one hand, we feel more "connected" to others than ever before, since we take information about their daily lives with us everywhere we go. And yet, that doesn't seem to be assuaging our loneliness but rather making it worse.

If this is you, might it be because you are performing and posing, rather than truly allowing yourself to be open enough to connect and be known? Might you be hiding your genuine self behind your idealized, filtered selfie?

Real connection involves imperfections, because it is authentic—and *we are imperfect*. Interactions and conversations that are the most intimate tend to involve some spontaneity; they are organic. You might snort, say the wrong thing, and see unexpected nuances. Real connection means that you have risked being the real you, in real time. And it seems so many more of us are scared of that.

The cultural norms of social media now pressure us to send out the equivalent of press releases about ourselves, about who we supposedly "are" as people. We want to carefully curate all of it, so we can get the "right" kind of validation and approval from our audience. We secretly want our online personas to sort of be us, but "better."

But that creates a barrier that walls off the *real* us. Of course we don't want to let all our imperfections hang out in front of hundreds of people—that's understandable. But if we carry this harsh, idealized standard into the way we think of ourselves, we're in trouble. And if it bleeds into the way we relate to the closest people in our lives—the ones who are supposed to get more than the press release, more than the filtered version of us—we've got no one left to love us for who we really are.

It is all too easy to become accustomed to the selfie smile, staged for the camera, rather than the smile that comes as a genuine reaction to something that brought us joy. In the past, those staged smiles were occasional, with a posed picture every few weeks or so. Now it's how many people live on a daily basis. *There's no longer a distinction between the staging and the experience. Performing is taking the place of being.*

How is all this affecting your self-talk, and your beliefs about who you are? How much of your true essence is now prohibited from connecting with others?

Opening Yourself Up to a Way Forward

We *can* get insight from digital relationships that are beautiful and intimate in their own right: the message board with others who experienced your same weird childhood, and who *get* it. The GoFundMe campaign that helps give a child a chance in life after tragedy strikes. The grandmother who videoconferences with her grandkids and delights in seeing them laugh at her corny jokes from 5,000 miles away. The person who finds solace in her Facebook friends' condolences and memories after she has lost her father.

What if you let the truest form of yourself be known, barriers down?

I mean the essence of your spirit, the heart that belongs to you and only you— whole and valid even in its imperfections. That self has a fundamental human need not just to be seen, but to be understood and loved. What if you expressed that and were treasured for it? That's the part of you that needs to be embraced so that you do not feel lonely. And satisfying that self is what creates the belongingness and community that truly combat not only loneliness but social anxiety. Whether you are online or in person.

Do you notice what all those situations have in common? The posing is gone. These individuals are pushing through the fear and letting themselves be vulnerable and authentic. What if you let yourself believe that being yourself is enough? It takes refusing to internalize the anxious voice, declining to "fix" yourself to be more digitally appealing or gain more of an audience. It means treating those urges as dysfunctional, negative self-talk—which you now have the tools to label and let pass.

Research backs me up on this. As much as we may want to group all online interactions into overly broad categories ("That's good," "That's bad," or "OK, that's just weird") there is a very wide spectrum of digital behavior. Passively scrolling through social media, clicking "like" here and there, is linked with feeling lonelier. These are considered "lightweight" interactions, and they probably just scratch a temporary itch rather than give us real emotional nourishment. But when we actively engage—write an individual message, type something personal to someone, have an actual back-and-forth interaction that feels more authentic and spontaneous—it can make us feel more connected.

Think about your habits online. Do you truly interact, or just react? Do you scroll mindlessly, alone, or do you build bonds and engage? Those latter activities push through the micro-bits of social anxiety. They give you the courage not just to perform, edit, and curate, but to truly be yourself.

Break Through the Perfect to Get to the Real

Do you know what decades of research have shown, time and time again, to be most helpful in combatting social anxiety?

You nudge yourself to breathe through it, building yourself up in the process. You learn that anxiety can be moved through, and that it's not all that scary after all—and that the interactions you were afraid of can end up feeling very rewarding. *You do the thing that scares you.*

I think it's time that this treatment mind-set helped more than just those with social anxiety disorder. I believe that for all of you struggling with disconnection, editing yourself, and over-preparing for your audience (because you're afraid that maybe the likes won't come otherwise), all leading to an awful lot of negative self-talk, this can work for you too.

This doesn't mean posting something online that will make people hate you. But it does mean going more for the spontaneous, organic connections that feel authentic and real: connections that are unedited, uncalculated, and unplanned.

There are plenty of small, everyday ways to choose this more genuine connection. Check out the examples on the next page that can add up to a big difference.

Opening ourselves up to more spontaneous, unplanned interactions is so hard for many of us. And if we can't do these things from behind a screen, it's even harder to do them in person. We just don't want to, which is why we tend to flake out on in-person social events more than ever before. Technology makes it so easy to cancel, even at the last minute, and social events feel so effortful, requiring so much work to get ourselves to go, to switch out of our day leggings and into our evening leggings. You may feel nervous about opening yourself up to the uncertainty of these unplanned interactions. You can't edit or filter a real-time outing. Living the moment somehow feels harder than producing it. And the less accustomed to just living you are, the scarier it is.

Choosing More Personal Connections

Instead of	*Consider This*
Clicking "like" for the seventh time in one minute	Choosing one of those people to message directly ("I was thinking of you the other day and wondering about X. How's it going?")
Looking down at your phone when someone enters the elevator	Making eye contact and smiling, even briefly with no conversation
Posting "HBD!" on a friend's social media feed on their birthday	Texting them a funny memory that the two of you shared as you wish them another great year
Spending five whole minutes choosing and editing a selfie	Seeing if you can cut it down to two minutes, and posting one that feels imperfect
Frequently posting declarations about things	Frequently asking questions and encouraging discussion
Reaching for your phone out of automatic habit	Creating a go-to list of other easy pastimes and relaxers (sudoku, crochet, listening to music, cuddling your pet, soaking your feet, or doing your favorite yoga pose)

But if you want to live as your whole, authentic self, open to other people and to life, you must break through the walls. You must let go and let pass the negative self-talk that says you're not good enough without filtering and editing. Yes, this means doing more stuff in your physical world: scheduling that lunch, putting your phone in your pocket at dinner and leaving it there, inviting people into your home, even if your kitchen predates Richard Nixon's administration. Remembering the name of the cashier who checks you out each week (research even says that small talk helps our mood as well, as much as some of you will fight me on that). Going around your office with some dough-nuts. Stopping the stage-managing of your life where you try to create scenes that are supposedly more interesting, pretty, humorous, or compelling. Refraining from removing yourself from the afterglow of a meaningful moment to immediately start crafting its description for social media.

You can also practice this online, and it's about being mind-ful. Not letting the automatic habit of scrolling be your perma-nent itch-scratch, but instead asking yourself the hard questions about what feelings you're trying to get—and what you're trying to run from. You've got to recognize that when social media makes you feel jealous, resentful, disconnected, or sad, or even just numb, it's not the best nourishment.

When you're presenting yourself online, see if you can allow yourself to just be—to value the truest, most complicated parts of yourself and not be ashamed of them, but to let them be seen and known. To truly interweave yourself with others, rather than just performing to get approval or acceptance. To truly express complicated emotions, rather than oversimplify them with emojis. It's about opening yourself up, listening, and being uncertain, rather than just posting declarations that are intended to shape what people think of you.

You've got to break through the perfect to get to the real—which is sometimes messy, but always more beautiful. If you really look at your behavior and see yourself scrolling over and over again, multiple times per hour, dozens of times per day, then try to ask yourself what you're looking for in those moments, and why that itch keeps coming back. What hole are you looking to fill? What gap are you looking to bridge?

And if that hole is within you, will putting up a wall in your interactions with others really help? Probably not. Ask yourself instead, how will you really connect in those moments when your need is strongest? How will you find for yourself what you are longing for? It's not that you have to give up social media. It's that you must be honest with yourself about the ways you use it. And you have to be willing to be *you*, even when it scares you. You have to ask yourself—especially, ironically, when social media feels like a little too much—is this *enough*?

Jessica and the Toxic Comparison

The problem of excessively comparing ourselves with others existed long before social media, although social media exacerbates it. My guess is that even in cave-dwelling days, people worried about whether their cave was as nicely decorated as their neighbor's.

Where does your idea of your own value come from? My client Jessica came to therapy after turning twenty-five and realizing she used herself as a "mental punching bag." She said unkind things to herself in the mirror each morning, she scrutinized pictures of herself with dismay, she constantly felt ashamed of her apartment, and she got major anxiety in certain social situations around her friends and family—even though she was fine at public speaking. She said at our first meeting, "It's strange. I wouldn't consider myself depressed—there's a lot of ways I love my life—and yet I've got a constant running commentary of all the ways I don't measure up."

"Measure up to what?" I asked.

"To everything," she said. "And everyone. When I'm out with my girlfriends I'm not thin enough or pretty enough. When I'm at a conference with my coworkers I'm not competent or smart enough. When I'm at Thanksgiving with my family I'm not accomplished enough. When I'm on a date I'm not interesting enough. Even in here . . ."

She stopped.

I opened up my face in a question.

"I don't know. I'm already wondering if you're going to think this is a silly reason for coming to therapy. Like I'm not as bad off as some people so why am I wasting our time. Like . . ." She smirked. "Like I'm not troubled enough."

We both allowed ourselves a chuckle, grinning at each other. "Like even feeling like you don't measure up, doesn't measure up," I said.

"Yes," she laughed, shaking her head at what she felt was the silliness of it all.

But it wasn't silly. It was a gnawing discomfort that had seeped into the way she lived her life, yet—with practice and time—she could finally free herself of it. First, she needed to learn what it was she was up against.

Torching the Yardstick

Somewhere along the way, Jessica had learned to use others as a yardstick. She viewed her own achievements, character traits, and even her appearance through the lens of how they compared with other people's.

This is a subtle habit that many of us don't even realize we are perpetuating, because the "others" we're comparing ourselves to have become completely internalized. Jessica kept dragging her feet on booking a beach vacation with her friends, for instance, because the idea of being in a swimsuit next to them was so uncomfortable. Maybe someday if she lost weight. But that strengthened the message that her body was not good enough as it was—that she was somehow unworthy—which prevented her from feeling fully whole in her body as she was. (It also denied her the sunshine and sweet-drink-with-umbrella, along with the stress relief, adventure, and mental break a vacation could give her, no matter her size.)

Or she would tell herself that her apartment wasn't nice enough to have guests over, which made her feel not only more negative about her own home (and guess what—she still had to live there!), but it also denied her the laughs, warmth, fun, and strengthened relationships that she could have had if she could just bring herself to extend the invitations *now*.

Learning that this yardstick was there, when it didn't deserve to be, was the first step for Jessica. But even more crucial was to begin to defuse from it, just like defusing from a dysfunctional thought pattern. She needed to separate herself from the assumed truth or validity of this yardstick by labeling it, acknowledging it, and watching its thought patterns pass.

She also had to be willing to be vulnerable enough to let a more genuine version of herself truly be seen by others: to connect to, rather than feel measured by, the people in her life who mattered.

We began to call this "Torching the Yardstick" (which sometimes she embraced as the command FTY: F___ the Yardstick.)

Torching the yardstick had many components, and most of them were small steps that added up to great strides over time. When Jessica had the thought on a phone call with her parents that she wasn't making them proud enough because she hadn't achieved what her brother had, she labeled it as her Yardstick Voice, an unreliable narrator, and pictured a big wooden stick that was slowly crumbling in flames as she breathed through it. When Yardstick Voice said, "Your skin's gross" as she looked in the mirror, she pictured the same flames—and added a more fulfilling, validating voice that said, "Yardstick Voice comes from Instagram filters and airbrushed magazines. My skin, and I, are real and alive."

The more she acknowledged Yardstick Voice, the more prevalent she realized it had been—and how deep-seated it had become. But something very interesting happened just as she began to feel a little despondent that the voice was more pervasive than she realized. She noticed that it didn't seem to bother her nearly as much anymore. Even though it was still around, it had lost a lot of its power to hurt her.

Homes, bodies, and money were Jessica's biggest insecurities, and they tend to be hot buttons culturally as well. Maybe you disappear from vacation photographs because you don't like the way you look (or might spend far too much time and frustration trying to get the perfect selfie with the perfect filter), or you might spend hours comparing your home negatively with others' homes, thinking that yours is not tidy/spacious/pretty enough. Or you wonder why Mike can afford that pool and you can't. You devalue yourself because of some supposed yardstick about what you (or your home, or your IRA) "should" look like, concluding that you don't "measure up."

But measure up to what, or to whom? There will always be someone richer, or whose house is nicer than ours, or who looks better in a swimsuit. We can choose to constantly feel "less than" because of this, or to live our lives. Why should other people's external appearances contain the grading scale for our self-worth, whether through their living rooms or their abs? No doubt there's a mansion or bank account or body somewhere that would put these *other* people to shame. So it could go on and on. Why give the power to some arbitrary ideal that has no bearing on whether you should feel valid, yourself? Why deny yourself the ability to appreciate yourself for who you are?

Frequently, these ideals are distorted anyway. We often compare our real lives to the idealized lives that others present externally. This is the proverbial comparing your *insides* with someone else's *outsides* (or, more specifically, comparing your insides to someone else's Instagram). You may think someone is happier, luckier, calmer, or more worry-free than you are, but in reality you have no idea. You know only what they present outwardly, and because of selective attention, you absorb more easily the things they present that match the beliefs you already hold. You think someone has the "perfect" marriage, an "easy" life, a "dream" job, a "lucky" break, or piles of cash—and you see their social media persona as evidence. But you have no idea what they're really feeling inside or what's going on behind the scenes—the same way you likely aren't being 100 percent real in the image you project either.

Imperfection Can Be Perfect

Thankfully, there is some cultural backlash to these perfectionistic yardsticks. We can Pinterest and Instagram our way into believing that our bodies and our hallways need forever to be picture-perfect, or we can embrace the insights of Allison Slater Tate, whose essay "The Mom Stays in the Picture" has resonated with many. In it, she describes her knee-jerk, familiar-to-most-women hesitation about getting into a picture with her kids when she was feeling particularly non-photogenic. (As social media becomes more widespread, the urge seems to be to overstage the perfect picture, to take time out of the real moment to make sure it appears as pretty as possible to others.) Tate ultimately comes to the conclusion that to worry about her appearance is missing the point—and it denies her something very important.

Because someday, she wants her kids to be able to look back at photos of the mom they loved: real photos. Photos that conveyed the way they looked at her and how she cared for them. Photos of her being alive, not living for the camera. Just as when she thought of her own mother, it wasn't about having the perfect hair, clothes, or body. It was about being with her, with all the joy and love and memories that represented their relationship. That was what was real.

To believe that you're not worthy of being in the picture is to subtly tell yourself that you're not worthy of even being in the moment: that you don't measure up; that you aren't deserving of fully experiencing the present. (This is just as harmful as the belief that an experience doesn't matter *unless* it is photographed, or staging every picture to "perfection" to the point where it isn't really capturing anything meaningful at all.)

As for the "perfect" home, thankfully, there's backlash there as well. "Scruffy Hospitality"—first named in an essay by the Reverend Jack King—refers to the willingness to embrace socializing over perfection, to prioritize togetherness over fretting about whether the silverware matches. A similar mind-set has given birth to "Crappy Dinner Parties"—the point being that such parties are not actually crappy at all; they only momentarily feel that way to the host who was preemptively fretting about the frayed tablecloth.

By pushing through the fretting, the host—and the guests—can reap tremendous rewards. Certainly, a fun dinner gathering, with all its "imperfections," is far better than no gathering at all. In fact, imperfections can bring humanity to a situation. Things going "wrong" can sometimes create funny stories for later. How much better to go ahead and create the memory to carry with you rather than being too frightened to have ever lived out the story in the first place.

Living for the experience—not its narration, or its comparison with others' experiences—is ultimately what a truly fulfilling life is made of.

Finding true connections instead of searching for approval

Nudge yourself toward being more open and vulnerable in your connections with others, which helps you better embrace and live your genuine life.

1 **REFLECT** on a high you've experienced in the past few months, where you felt joy, pride, wonder, awe, or humor. Who did you share it with, and how? Did it help you feel connected, or did you find yourself trying to craft it for an audience? Scroll through your social media and look for your patterns and themes. What do your posts seem to seek? What narrative are you creating, and how close does that feel to the real you? How do high (or low) numbers of "likes" affect how you view what's important in your life?

2 **ASK** yourself: Are you lonely? If so, think about when you feel less lonely, and what makes those times different. How can you increase those experiences? Might it be time to put more energy or time into building new relationships, repairing ones that have acquired cracks, or improving ones that have faded? Are there small habits you can acquire to help you feel more connected on a daily basis?

3 **CATCH** yourself slipping into patterns of comparison. Do you invoke a yardstick that has no business being there? Do you think of your own value only as it compares with other people? Counteract these moments by labeling the anxious, dysfunctional thinking. It will get in your way only if you engage with it and let it stick.

You've Absorbed False Meanings for Gratitude and Forgiveness

GRATITUDE AND FORGIVENESS ARE MORE than just memes—both are correlated with decreased depression and anxiety. Forgiveness is associated with improved mental and physical well-being, and gratitude boosters—from meditation to writing a well-thought-out thank-you note—provide a measurable mood boost as well.

But practicing gratitude and forgiveness is much easier said than done, especially because some of us (let's admit it now!) aren't even on board with the concepts. It sure can ring false to summon a thank-you to the universe when you've had an absolutely horrible day. And who's in the mood to be grateful when they've got a health concern or a terrible boss, or the world feels like a cesspool of misery? Why would you decide to forgive someone who has hurt you, when you're still feeling the negative ripple effects?

In these moments, finding gratitude or forgiveness can seem trite and ring hollow, at best. At worst, it feels infuriating and invalidating, like being told how to feel.

But that's because our traditional notions of gratitude and forgiveness are a little out of whack. You may have been taught as a child that gratitude meant stuffing your upset ("Stop whining! Lots of kids don't even have a roof over their heads. You have nothing to complain about!") or that forgiveness meant erasing any memory of harm done to you ("Your sister apologized! Forgive her and forget about it!"). But neither of these are part of the true, more nuanced concepts of forgiveness and gratitude that are so beneficial to our mental health. So let's get some myths out of the way.

If you want to face your life with the type of gratitude that is so beneficial—the grateful heart and open eyes that are so highly associated with that elusive peaceful soul—you must make the choice to be present for both the light and the darkness. Being grateful means that you recognize that all parts of your life belong to the same whole, even when they are scary or sad, disappointing or maddening. Related to our discussion of sublimation in Chapter 4, gratitude isn't forcing yourself to be happy that your heart is broken. It's being willing to understand that a broken heart nonetheless still beats, and even has special depth to it.

Just as the false version of gratitude forces you to feel a certain way, so too does false forgiveness. And myths about forgiveness can be even more dangerous. So let's clear them up.

The Truth of Gratitude

Gratitude Is Not . . .	Gratitude Is . . .
"Counting your blessings" in a way that ignores the crappy stuff	Being attuned to the whole picture of your life in an open-minded way, with humility and compassion
Comparing your plight with that of others and saying you don't have a right to feel upset	Recognizing that pain is inseparable from the experience of life
Forcing yourself to be happy when you're feeling discontented	Honoring the lessons, insights, and wisdom that have come from all your experiences, including negative ones
Insisting on finding a silver lining to erase the dark cloud	Having hope for the sunrise, even in the darkest hour of night; and being willing to search for beauty and love even in experiences you hate
Being appreciative of others to the point of ignoring things that need to be changed in their behavior	Deciding that engaging with life, being fully immersed in it and letting yourself feel even the difficult parts, beats the alternative of running from it

The Truth of Forgiveness

Forgiveness Is Not . . .	Forgiveness Is . . .
Telling someone it's OK they did what they did, or automatically accepting their apology	Letting go of the need to "make things even" through revenge or retribution
Giving someone permission to harm you again	Granting yourself permission to no longer carry the burden of hate toward someone else
Forgetting the warning signs you've taken from a bad experience	Allowing yourself to take your own meaning from an experience, not necessarily what someone else thinks you should take from it
Releasing someone who has harmed you from a rightful consequence, punishment, or justice	Releasing yourself from continuing to resent someone when it no longer serves your own needs
Being "all right" with the fact that something happened or was done to you	Believing that you deserve to move forward from pain

Much as true gratitude does not involve ignoring pain, forgiveness does not mean ignoring that something was done to you, or allowing yourself to be pressured to reconcile with the person who harmed you. Just because you work toward forgiveness of someone does not mean that you have to let them back into your life. And it doesn't have to be contrary to seeing justice served. (Sadly, some people think that forgiveness means that a person should keep quiet about abuse they have suffered at someone's hands, even when they want to speak out. This is misguided and harmful, and is not likely to bring the psychological benefits of true forgiveness.)

But let's understand the difference between justice and revenge. Justice sets things right, or as right as possible. Revenge prolongs a cycle of pain and hate. Forgiveness involves relinquishing hate and the need for revenge—but it need not involve abandoning the fight for justice.

Forgiveness means releasing the burden of resentment that's been compounding and perpetuating your hurt. Of course, resentment and even hate can be natural—for a while. But they are often kept alive because we feel that's the only way to remember what was done to us. We fear that if we truly forgive, then we'll forget as well.

But forgiveness allows you to remember. And in reality, it gives you more control of your story, freeing you from perpetually being harmed anew by the same pain. As the saying goes, hate eventually corrodes its container.

Starting the Process

So gratitude and forgiveness both involve finding ways to take in the big picture of your life, eventually reaching peace with the whole of it. Gratitude and forgiveness release you from the struggle of trying to make things become something they are not (and cannot be).

That means that the early steps look similar to the work you're already doing with learning to face uncomfortable feelings. So if you are struggling with these newer concepts of gratitude and forgiveness, revisiting the older ones in Chapter 5 about sitting with difficult emotions will be helpful. Think about making a conscious effort to be more willing to engage with life rather than running from its difficult parts, to lean into a given experience as a whole, discomfort and all. Keep working not to run from negative thoughts, but instead to learn to see them, label them, and let them pass.

Now, let's add empathy and compassion to the mix.

The Role of Empathy

Empathy at its heart is being open to considering and even sharing the emotional experience of someone else. It's not just imagining how someone else may be feeling ("If that happened to me, I'd be livid!"), but it is letting that perspective evoke something in you ("I remember what it was like when I lost my own father—ugh, I am just so sad for her right now"). It's being willing to walk the proverbial mile in someone else's shoes, no matter how dirty, tight, or straight-from-the-trends-of-1992 those shoes are.

People who are empathetic aren't just more likely to have better relationships, and be more sensitive and caring partners, friends, and coworkers. They also have an easier time with forgiveness, which helps them too. Remember, forgiveness is not about making excuses for someone else or letting them off the hook unnecessarily. It's about realizing that your hurt does not exist in a vacuum, but instead is part of a larger universe that connects you to others.

To help free yourself from the suffering that someone has caused you, choose at least to attempt to acknowledge their own pain, vulnerability, or emotional battles. Once again, this does not mean condoning the fact that they wronged you. (So many people think that empathizing means making excuses for someone, just as they assume forgiveness means forgetting the offensive actions in the first place. But it's much more profound than that, and far more beautiful.)

This can bring relief in the moment, and has even been shown to slow the aging process. As counterintuitive and difficult as it may seem, might you consider sending a healing thought to a person who harmed you? Are you willing to (even temporarily) take a more holistic perspective, deciding that this person having less of a struggle is helpful to the energy of the world as a whole? Are you willing to add a little smidgen of compassion into the universe, understanding that this can come back to you as well?

Maybe this just feels too hard. I understand. You may still very much want the person to "pay" by suffering. If that's the case, let's start smaller. Choose to put forth empathy not for the person who did the greatest harm to you, but rather the person who cut you off in traffic, for instance. After all, you don't know the real story there, right? Maybe they were on the way to see their dying mother, or were exhibiting the very worst symptoms of food poisoning, right there on the highway. What if you sent them a simple thought: "I hope your struggle gets easier"?

Your own struggle with this may feel like too much. It may feel too counterintuitive or difficult. There is no judgment here if you choose not to try this yet. But if you do, and you begin to practice it regularly, you will likely be surprised by how it helps you heal, releasing anger bit by bit.

This is related to a Sanskrit concept called "ahimsa" that is reflected in a variety of cultures, faiths, and social movements. Gandhi practiced it and inspired others to follow. Aspects of it can be seen in Dr. Martin Luther King Jr.'s leadership and the nonviolent protests of the civil rights movement. Ironically, it was first introduced to me by my own therapist (yup!) at a time in my life where I habitually blamed and punished myself for things that were out of my control.

That brings us to something that many of us struggle with: self-forgiveness. In the depths of emotional darkness, sometimes it's not about other people at all. It's about ourselves.

When Beating Yourself Up Feels Less Scary Than the Alternative

Blaming yourself may be far easier, and come more naturally, than facing your fears. Take thirty-one-year-old Julianne. Julianne's twin sister, Rebecca—a creative, vibrant, and loving person—lived out a tragic struggle with opioid addiction. Rebecca spiraled downward for years before dying of a heroin overdose, the day after Julianne had confronted her about getting help and Rebecca had denied that she needed it.

Julianne was despondent with guilt and blamed herself. This hijacked her thoughts and mood virtually every day, adding to the devastating grief she was already dealing with. Not only could Julianne not forgive herself for Rebecca's death, she would not have even identified self-forgiveness as a goal. She did not believe that she deserved it.

Ahimsa basically means this: We are all connected, and to hurt another being is, in essence, to hurt oneself.

And it goes both ways. Just as seeking violent revenge on someone who harmed you will likely end up hurting you in the long run, beating yourself up over and over for something is also putting more harm back into the universe. In any given moment, you can add to the world's pain, or add to its compassion. Which do you choose?

Though Julianne had tried for years to get help for Rebecca, she felt certain she hadn't done enough. In her mind, there was always "one more thing" she could have done, especially in the weeks leading up to Rebecca's death. She should have forced Rebecca to stay overnight with her, even if the confrontation got physical. She should have found Rebecca's dealer and threatened to call the police. She should have confiscated Rebecca's cell phone. She should have taken a leave of absence from her job to be with Rebecca nonstop. She should have hired someone to strong-arm Rebecca into another attempt at rehab. She should have offered Rebecca a bribe—any bribe, Julianne's life savings if necessary—to force her to go to inpatient treatment. (Julianne also felt certain that her actual confrontation with Rebecca is what killed her, and that she should have just stayed quiet in that particular moment. So she beat herself up from both sides.) The list of "shoulds" went on.

Of course, this list defied logic. Even if Rebecca had stayed with Julianne, as she had in the past, she could have sought heroin while Julianne was sleeping, as she had in the past. Should Julianne have never slept? Rebecca had multiple dealers and multiple "friends" who would pick her up and supply drugs. There was no way at that point to cut them off unless Rebecca chose to. Rebecca had also occasionally disappeared or gotten physically aggressive with Julianne when she tried to set limits. What if Julianne herself got hurt—how would she have kept Rebecca safe then? What if Julianne had depleted her savings—and Rebecca still did not get clean? And what evidence was there that doing *nothing* instead of the confrontation that day would have ended Rebecca's addiction and kept her alive? Addiction, not a confrontation, killed Rebecca. Of course the "shoulds" weren't rational.

But something else far more important began to emerge as we worked together: Julianne had a strong, unconscious motive to keep blaming herself. By telling herself that she caused Rebecca's death, Julianne kept some control. The world could still be a fair and just place—Julianne simply hadn't done what she was *supposed to*. In this version, had Julianne followed a concrete series of steps, then Rebecca would still be alive. *The universe could still make sense.*

Unfortunately, life is more unpredictable—and potentially frightening—than that. And that was what Julianne was choosing to avoid thinking about. Blaming herself was actually more comfortable.

Julianne and her husband had been starting to talk about having children. The root of her negative self-talk became clear: If Julianne believed that she could have stopped Rebecca from dying, then she could also believe she'd be able to keep her future children safe from harm as well.

By holding on to her blame, Julianne protected herself against something far darker: the terrifying reality that addiction is brutal, ugly, and unfair, and can kill someone you've loved since the day they were born. That you can try and try to get someone help, but when they refuse it, you can't control their behavior, even when you want desperately to save them. That loving someone opens you up to a staggering amount of emotional risk, and choosing to be a parent makes this risk chronic and unrelenting.

This reality—especially given Julianne's grief—was absolutely paralyzing. It was far "easier" to imagine that she could have saved Rebecca, that it was Julianne's own mistakes that led to her death. Because, at least in that world, Julianne could avoid making the same "mistakes" with her own children someday.

Holding On to Blame to Run from Our Fears

This dynamic is not nearly as uncommon as you'd think. And it doesn't show up only with self-blame: We also tend to more harshly blame *others* because of our desire to see the world as predictable, fair, and orderly. It feels easier and more comfortable to believe that someone deserved the awful thing that happened to them, rather than understanding that sometimes awful things happen, and they can happen to *us* too. Awful things can strike like lightning out of the blue, even when we've followed the rules—and this can terrify us. How much more convenient and comforting to assume that people who fall victim to terrible things must have had it coming. By believing that life is predictable, and that terrible things happen only to people who have done something wrong, we don't have to face the far scarier truth: Sometimes life brings unexpected pain even to people who have done everything right and don't deserve it at all.

Blame, though, blocks out the chance for connection.

And acknowledging our deepest fears is what lets in the light. In Julianne's case, once we uncovered the fears underneath the blame, we could finally start addressing them. Not only could we find better ways for her to manage those fears going forward, and healthy ways to cope with the unpredictable scariness of life (and parenting), but we could also, finally, help Julianne see the truth—that she was not responsible for Rebecca's death. And she could begin to truly reckon with the full tragedy of the loss and stop hiding from it by making it about her own "mistakes." Only then could Julianne start to grieve

Rebecca in a pure, whole, genuine way—not a contorted one full of layers of anger at herself.

It took time and was scary at first, but Julianne was finally able to let go of the blame and rumination. She could label those fears and anxious thoughts as what they truly were, and understand that they didn't represent truth—and that she didn't have to run from them anymore. She could finally, with work and insight, give herself permission to set down the self-punishment, to free herself from carrying it any longer.

She could forgive herself.

When You Truly Have Hurt Others

All right, you may be saying. *Julianne could forgive herself because Rebecca's death really wasn't her fault. What about something that really was my fault? Like a mistake that really did harm other people? How do you come to a place of forgiveness for that?*

Guilt over seriously harming someone else can be debilitating, and even lead to self-destructive behavior. The physical effects of guilt are substantial; it's associated with higher rates of heart problems and high blood pressure. It's tempting to refuse to forgive yourself, as a form of penance. To believe that staying miserable is the proper way to atone for what you have done.

But let's challenge that for a moment. First, coming to a place of self-forgiveness and ultimately carrying your regret differently is not unduly letting yourself off the hook. Nor is it denying that you did anything wrong. Rather, it is growing from it. And that growth helps you move forward and allows you to put further good back into the world.

If you refuse ever to come to a place of self-forgiveness, it is hard to imagine how you'll be able to be a fully open, positive person, engaging with other people in the ways that a kind, compassionate life calls for. Instead, you will be walled off from others, hiding behind your own pain and the need to punish yourself. But by finding meaning in your transgression and moving forward, rather than being paralyzed by regret, you can make a clearer plan to truly atone through your actions, rather than merely beating yourself up about it for years on end.

Return to the exercises in Chapter 6 that help you find meaning in your regrets, many of which will be helpful even when those regrets involve the shame and guilt of harming someone else. Finding meaning to carry forward from your mistake helps the self-forgiveness process.

Apologizing—truly and vulnerably, even if it is not "accepted"—can be an important part of the self-forgiveness process. So too can talking through with others the realities of what you have done, whether with friends, family, or a professional. Owning your experience out loud helps clarify it and keeps you from retreating constantly into your misery as a way of avoiding moving forward. This allows you to improve your connection with others, and to better understand that no life is completely free from suffering. (Of course, be cautious that talking to others doesn't just turn into beating yourself up over and over again. It should be about releasing yourself, not entrapping yourself further.)

Finally, thinking about how to do good for others—even if they are not the ones directly hurt by you—can help you forgive yourself. Supporting others not only provides a mood boost, but it can restore your faith in your ability to put positivity back into the world. Gratitude is useful here as well. The more you can practice gratitude for your life's big picture, the more you can accept the full reality of it—including your mistakes.

Shame, humiliation, guilt—they can pack the most intense of emotional punches. Maybe they've even been absorbed into who you are, to the point where you can't imagine their not being a part of you. Perhaps you can't fathom ever releasing yourself from that pain.

Perhaps you don't even feel you'd deserve that release anyway. But if it's helpful to show empathy and compassion to others, how could it possibly be unhelpful to show that to yourself?

Confronting Negative Self-Talk about the Past

Maybe your need for self-forgiveness is not about one huge thing, but a chronic, unrelenting series of little ones. People with social anxiety are particularly prone to this. They may become trapped in a cycle of rumination about the past (*Why did I say that? I can't believe I did that. I bet they got mad at me but didn't let on. I wonder if they're talking about it behind my back*). And this can lead to feelings of shame, guilt, and even depression (whereas worries about the *future* tend to bring fear and dread).

But the worries-about-the-past cycle has many similarities with the worries-about-the-future cycle. It's replaying something in your head over and over, giving it the power to stick. And these ruminations don't provide clarity, insight, or strength. Label them as hecklers in your mental audience. And as any stand-up comedian has had to learn, the more you go back-and-forth with a heckler, the louder and more obnoxious they become. If you totally ignore them, they take it as a challenge to make themselves heard. In the end, a brief acknowledgment without positive reinforcement—establishing that the heckling is not a valid part of the real act happening onstage, the act that's about to go on now, thank you very much—is the way to go.

Discovering a true sense of gratitude and forgiveness

Allow yourself to build new understanding of what gratitude, empathy, and forgiveness can mean to you, and how you can incorporate them into your life to reap their benefits.

1 **NAME** a person, maybe even yourself, whom you've had a hard time forgiving. Sit for three minutes and attempt to empathize with that person or send them calm, healing thoughts. If that feels difficult, envision just sending those calm, healing thoughts into the world at large.

2 **INHALE** deeply through your nose, with a slow, long exhale out through your mouth. Attempt to visualize something that symbolizes your whole life—an orb, a timeline, an hourglass, a river, anything that comes to mind. Now, imagine it as a true whole—making sure to include the messy, embarrassing, and painful parts, and all the regrets, guilt, and parts you'd normally be tempted to erase or forget. Visualize your life as an entirety, each part of it inseparable from the rest, worthy as is and valid unconditionally.

3 **SIT** with that visual of your life and breathe with it for a few minutes. Let it become part of you as you view it with as much openhearted acceptance as you can muster. Revel in the fact that it is in you, and you are in it—and you are truly, fully alive.

PART IV

Your Future

"For us, there is only the trying. The rest is not our business."

T. S. ELIOT

9

You Give Too Much Power to "Willpower" and "Goals"

WILLPOWER: IT'S SUPPOSED TO HELP us with everything from motivation for doing the dishes to withstanding the power of the autoplay during our Netflix binge. (*Just. One. More.*) But I strongly believe that our cultural worship of willpower is one more symptom of something that by now you know well: We give far too much power to our thoughts.

The central idea of willpower is that our thoughts must be "strong" enough. That if our minds take on the sleek, hairless musculature of a champion bodybuilder, then our behavior—anything we want—will fall into place. *Our thoughts will make it happen!* (Sound familiar?) With that classic American can-do spirit, we believe we can motivate ourselves into or out of anything, if only we have the right attitude. Never mind our circumstances; never mind our environments; never mind that chocolate fudge torte staring at us from the kitchen counter. We should be able to overcome it all, just by the power of our will alone.

As we've discussed, it seems inspiring to believe that all we have to do is think something, and we make it happen: weight loss, quitting a vice, getting a new career. But it's not so inspiring when we set ourselves up for failure. We're putting ourselves at the mercy of our thoughts: thoughts that often refuse to do what we tell them to, on principle. And the related idea—that if we don't achieve good things in life, it's because our thoughts "failed," as we didn't have the adequate strength of mind—is even more damaging. This tells us that maybe we really didn't want it enough or, even worse, we are just weak.

But as we've established, being subservient to our thoughts is no way to live an autonomous, active life. We can choose instead merely to observe our thoughts, and act completely differently from them. It's not just your immediate, conscious thoughts and visualizations that have to determine your behavior.

You are more than your conscious thoughts.

But real behavior change also involves factors we don't always like to acknowledge. Thoughts seem almighty in part because we want to believe that as humans, our minds operate on a different level. Most of us don't want to think that the processes that make our dog learn to sit, a rat press a lever, or a seal perform on cue are the same ones that could apply to our own behavior, shaping our lives and relationships. Surely we're too sophisticated to respond to such basic behavioral principles. We're far more complex than the dog, the rat, or the seal.

And in many ways we *are* more sophisticated than those animals. But even though our brains are capable of higher-order thinking, there are fundamental behavioral principles that apply across the board to all animals, us former cave-dwellers included. Let's look at some of those now.

We Need Reinforcement to Keep Doing Something

We keep going to work because it brings a paycheck. Slot machines are compelling because we occasionally get a payout (or think we have the chance to). In general, a behavior becomes reinforced—and more likely to be performed again—because we get something out of it. Maybe it's relief from discomfort (technically called negative reinforcement, if you'll let me wonk out for a minute here—since we're *removing* the reinforcement of the discomfort) or maybe it actively makes us feel good (like that paycheck or those jazzy bells going off on a slot machine called Cash Stampede).

If you're looking to pick up a new habit, you'll help yourself immensely by adding reinforcement. Sure, for some people, "I am proud of myself" is sufficient reinforcement, but most of us need something more tangible. But that thing doesn't have to undermine the goal or take away our intrinsic motivation for it. I don't recommend "I stuck to this miserable eating plan for five days; now I get to 'cheat' for the next two" as the reinforcement, because the key is to work in the same direction as the ultimate goal, not against it. And it's important to not make the reinforcement totally detached from the behavior, where it becomes the sole reason for it (like the kids whose grades tank once their parents stop paying for As).

Instead, find ways to bring positive reinforcement into the activity itself. Don't postpone and isolate the reward, which would make the activity feel even more like a dreadful slog you must be through with in order to finally feel good again. Aim for the behavioral equivalent of putting some greens in a tropical smoothie, rather than eating one leaf of greens in order to reward yourself with a carton of ice cream afterward.

Here are some ideas for working in those greens:

FOR DIMINISHING YOUR SPENDING: Create low-spending days where you actively seek out entertaining activities that are free or low-cost, and reserve them as treats for those days. This beats just doing a spending moratorium, because it reinforces the low-spending days as times that can feel good in their own right.

FOR EATING MORE HEALTHFULLY: Embrace making the healthy food more enjoyable in the moment, not only by making it prettier and seeking out truly tasty recipes, but by making sure you're particularly hungry when you eat it. Since having hunger satiated is a pleasurable sensation, this increases your satisfaction with the healthy stuff over time and positively reinforces it.

FOR BEING MORE CONSCIENTIOUS WITH HOUSEHOLD CHORES: If you can inject even the tiniest game or party vibe into a home maintenance task, it makes it easier—and more likely to get done quickly. When putting away dishes I'll estimate the number of forks to see how close I get, or time myself to see if I can beat the record for getting the plates done. Or as I pass through the kitchen, I'll pick a random number of things to put away in one go ("Count down just eleven items, then you can get that glass of water you wanted"). The drudgery of cleaning is brightened by making it more celebratory: Put on loud, energetic dance music, set up a hamper or recycling bin to shoot three-pointers into, spray words or silly pictures on your windows with cleaning solution before you wipe them down. Does this sound goofy? Absolutely. But is goofy more interesting than the same old same old, and will it make the time go faster? The answer is almost always yes.

We Avoid What We Fear

Not only do we tend to seek out what feels good, but we tend to avoid what raises our anxiety. You've probably seen some examples:

"I'm not going to go to the doctor. I might learn that I have some terrifying disease."

"I'm not going to cut down on my drinking. My social life might suffer and I'll be bored and lonely."

"I'm not going to tell my partner my true feelings. That might change the way they feel about me."

But what about when you don't even realize you're avoiding something? You can sabotage yourself even more when there is unacknowledged fear buried beneath something you think you want. Because if you don't recognize the fear, you can't address it. You'll get trapped and feel stuck, not realizing that you're scared, unable to understand why you keep dragging your feet on your goals.

Psychotherapy pioneer Alfred Adler exemplified this with his "magical question" exercise. Let's say there's a goal you really want to meet, yet you just can't seem to. You procrastinate and sabotage yourself at every turn. Well, Adler would say, "Let's say I had a magic wand," and with one wave of the wand, your goal would automatically be met.

It's been achieved. Done.

So here's Adler's question: *What would your life look like then?* If you finally achieved what you wanted, how would things be?

Let's say your goal was to finally complete your graduate degree—you've been in school *forever*. Yet you just can't seem to finish your thesis. You procrastinate, drag your feet, and never prioritize it. But at the same time, you feel desperate to finally be done with school, and can't understand what your problem is. (Maybe you say, "I need more willpower!") So when Adler's question is asked—what would your life look like if you finally finished your thesis—you can barely catch your breath. "That's what I've always wanted," you gush. "I'd finally be on my way to independent adulthood. I could get a real job. I'd be done with school, finally. Family members would stop asking me about my thesis. Maybe I'd even have time to date, and meet someone. I could maybe think about buying a place and settling down. I could stop buying ramen in a crinkly package and buy ramen in a restaurant."

Well, *that*, Adler would say, is what you're truly afraid of.

Maybe you're not finishing your thesis because you've gotten too comfortable. The misery of graduate school is still less anxiety-provoking than the unknown of the future. In fact, maybe you're truly scared of the "real world" future, since you've been in school so long. The idea of the responsibilities and decisions that come with it are frightening. A serious relationship? A mortgage? A job that requires wearing real pants? (*What are real pants?*) Having to *choose* the toppings on your ramen? It's nothing you've ever done before, and although you most definitely want to meet this goal, a significant part of you resists it, *because you are afraid of it*. And so you self-sabotage and procrastinate. Continually.

We avoid what we fear. But only once you understand what you're really afraid of can you devise a plan to face the fear and keep moving toward what you really want. Otherwise you will keep avoiding it—even when you don't realize that's what you're doing.

Procrastination Born Out of Fear

Procrastination is emblematic of this fear-avoidance problem. Sure, many times we procrastinate on things we just don't want to do (hello, taxes!). But other times, we procrastinate on things that we really do want to do—or at least we think we do. But we are scared, deep down, of their consequences.

When I work with someone who says they suffer from pro-crastination, it's imperative we figure out what's behind it. No two procrastinators are exactly alike. And there's a huge variety of outcomes, and severity, among procrastinators. Some need a little extra adrenaline in order to be energized to do their best work, so they wait until the last minute, but consistently knock the task out of the park. That's still pretty functional. Others keep disappointing their boss by asking to push back a deadline, feeling more and more miserable in the process and ultimately not getting the job done at all. That's pretty dysfunctional, and likely stems from fear. It's not really about willpower at all.

People who tend toward perfectionism (or are perfect at it!) are hit with this a lot.

They worry that if they don't get the job done perfectly, they'll let themselves or others down. And who wants to run full steam ahead into that discomfort? So the perfectionistic procrastinators put off the task. Waiting until the very last minute gives the added bonus of a ready excuse if their work fails to live up to their (or their boss's) standards. They protect their ego by reminding themselves they did it in only eight hours rather than eight days. (*So of course it wasn't my best work.*) They're refusing to fully step into the ring and make themselves vulnerable. If they lose, they want it to be by forfeit, not by knockout.

Another reason we procrastinate is because we have set goals that just don't work for us. Goals can be weighty in our minds, and they're all over our culture: They're a hashtag, an assignment from your boss, a page in your sister's blinged-out journal. Setting goals can be so beneficial, motivating us to do the things we need to do, and to achieve the dreams that matter most to us. But goal-setting is also an area of our lives that is rife with self-sabotage, a place where even the best of intentions can translate immediately into failure and hopelessness. Which is why we sometimes need to adjust them.

Adjusting Our Goal-Setting

Yup, I'll say it—a lot of us would be better off making zero goals whatsoever than sticking with the craptacular ones we tend to latch onto. But happily, adjusting our goal-setting is pretty straightforward. Let's take a look.

GOALS NEED TO BE SPECIFIC AND CONCRETE

UH-OH: Be more social.

YES: Invite someone to something two times this month.

The most intimidating tasks are often ones that are poorly defined. "Be better about money." "Improve my relationships." "Get healthy." "Find a new job." What do those really *look* like? Sometimes life throws these types of goals at you to check off your list: complex, multifaceted work projects. Figuring out what's wrong with your steering wheel and finding someone to repair it. Taking care of everything that needs to be done for the holidays. Such goals are hard to get hold of and find motivation to start, because they feel complicated and shapeless. Where do you get a toehold? Yet they carry a lot of weight, which is why I call them amorphous blobs.

But even the blobbiest of goals can be broken down into parts. Choose the most concrete, specific first step—even if it's "Find my old résumé file, open it, and rename it"—and start there.

GOALS NEED TO BE
MANAGEABLE AND REALISTIC

UH-OH: Reorganize my whole house.

YES: Purge two bags of clothes from my bedroom closet.

Many of us would like nothing more than to reorganize our entire home, exercise seven days a week, or eliminate all sugar from our diets. Scratch that—many of us would like nothing more than to *be the type of person who does these things*. But most of us just aren't going to. Not necessarily because we don't have the motivation, but because they're just not things we can realistically fit into our lives. (Remember: It's not about willpower.) So when we set goals like that, we're relying on magically becoming a whole new type of person, revamping our lives completely to accommodate fifty hours' worth of decluttering or a totally new sleep schedule that allows us to go to a gym. Why set ourselves up for failure like that?

Here's the thing: You need not declutter your whole home all at once (sorry, Marie Kondo!) to get a major boost to your space and well-being. You need not exercise seven or even five days a week in order to boost your health significantly. And—ironically—when you choose these extreme goals, that will likely prevent you from making any progress at all. "The perfect is the enemy of the good" is frequently said for a reason: It's very often true. Or my personal favorite, "If it's worth doing, it's worth doing poorly" (though that may not necessarily apply to brain surgery), gets at this too: You've got to remove the intimidation of taking the first step. If a first step is small or imperfect, that's OK—because at least it gets done and brings momentum. And with momentum, you can build something great, and realistic—that truly gets done.

GOALS NEED TO BE DEFINED BY EFFORT, NOT RESULTS

UH-OH: Lose ten pounds.

YES: Do twenty minutes of cardio twice a week, and eat a bag of greens per week.

A classic goal—particularly on January 1 when people are coming off a season of eggnog, cheese platters, and chocolate (the holy trinity!)—is this: "Lose weight." This of course runs afoul of the specific, concrete requirement we just discussed, so let's say you've heeded that and changed it to "Lose ten pounds." Well, the problem now is that this focuses on results, not effort.

You have more direct control over your precise efforts than you do your precise results. You can exercise X number of days per week, or eat Y servings of veggies per day. But it is harder to quantify exactly what it will take to lose ten pounds, so you're more likely to get lost on the way. (*How much longer will this take? If I'm not there yet, am I failing? I've been trying so hard and feeling good about myself, but it doesn't seem to be working.*) A hyper-focus on results can make you give up, especially if something is misleadingly masking the progress you've made (hello, water bloat!). But focusing on your efforts gives you a more helpful measure of what you're working toward.

GOALS NEED TO BE TIME-LIMITED

UH-OH: Quit biting nails.

YES: Spend two weeks chewing a chew necklace instead of my nails whenever it occurs to me.

Quitting a habit is a classic on the goal-setting greatest hits station. Whether it is nail-biting, buying high-priced coffee, or saying "I'm sorry" too much, it's very common to aspire to remove a "negative" habit. The biggest downfall here is denying yourself the opportunity to get a pat on the back, because such goals can never technically be reached. After all, what does "quit biting my nails" mean, specifically? When will you ever know that you've met that goal—someday on your deathbed when you haven't gnawed on them for decades? When you've substituted in a different habit that you like more? When you've finally been able to grow nails long enough that people don't automatically assume you've been spending time in a medieval torture device?

Being specific in your goals matters not just for their clarity, but also for their manageability. People in substance abuse recovery learn early on that they need to take their sobriety one day at a time, rather than staring at the intimidating vastness of the weeks, months, and years ahead. But habits far less life-or-death than sobriety can benefit from the exact same mind-shift. A day, week, or month of abstaining from an undesired habit are all worth celebrating. Don't deny yourself that opportunity by trying to "quit" something without an objective way to measure your success.

GOALS NEED TO HAVE A CLEAR PATHWAY

UH-OH: Get promoted at work this year.

YES: Solicit specific feedback from supervisor about what is needed, and bring at least one new idea to each meeting.

Having proper pathways to meet your goals is crucial; how will you know what to do otherwise? In fact, having realistic, workable pathways to meet goals boosts your hope and motivation to work toward them, as shown by the research of the late C. R. (Rick) Snyder. Make sure that your goal—even if it seems well-defined, like getting a specific raise or new title at work—is accompanied by a true and specific understanding of what you actually need to do to make this goal happen.

Otherwise, you have no road map (or GPS!), and you're bound to waste time with wrong turns.

THE CLEAN SLATE TRAP:
A LICENSE TO PROCRASTINATE

Tomorrow is by definition never here yet, and yet we often save all our best intentions for it. How many times have you slacked off at work from morning through lunch—feeling unproductive and sluggish—and then decided that the whole day was a wash and you'd start fresh tomorrow? (You might also recognize some all-or-none thinking there.) Or it's already Wednesday night and you haven't exercised all week, so you might as well "restart" next week?

But next week, there will likely be another reason to push things back, even if we assume we'll magically be more moti-vated. (We are notoriously bad at these predictions, called affective forecasting, as studied by Daniel Gilbert.) Months can go on this way. Granted, you can't necessarily do this at your workplace or you'll eventually get fired, but for goals that are personal, it is all too easy to string together years of avoidance. Tomorrow gets pushed back farther and farther, and never actually arrives.

Relying on the calendar to create a "clean slate" is often a trap. *You* should be the one to choose when you start something, not the clock. And you can do it whenever you want. A healthy choice made on a Thursday at 7:51 p.m. is just as valuable, or effective, as one made on Monday at 8:02 a.m.

If you continually refuse the opportunity right in front of you, because you want a rounder number via a certain date or a time, your goal only becomes farther away instead of closer. The opportunity of the moment you're in is always yours for the taking: right here, right now. Tomorrow may appear bright and shiny, but it's never inherently worthier than today. In fact, today has fewer unknowns—so it may even be a safer bet when getting started on something important. And it's one more day you will have under your belt when measuring your progress.

Plus, buying into the idea of tomorrow's "fresh start" or "clean slate" implies that your past and even present moments are somehow dirty. It's black-or-white thinking, and it takes away your ability to be flexible in appreciating your life as a whole. It creates false divisions that don't do you any favors.

Of course, sometimes there *are* specific days that matter immensely and truly mark a difference in a life. Getting sober, for instance. But that's a clean slate because of behavior—someone's actions going forward *made* that day mean something. The clean slate trap, on the other hand, would mean that you forever put off getting sober. You use your drug of choice for one "last" binge every night, while constantly convincing yourself you'll start fresh the next day. And unfortunately, that day never comes.

If you absolutely must have a clean slate to get motivated, create it mindfully, with as much autonomy as possible. Don't just default to tomorrow (or next week, month, or a new year). Why not have that clean slate start in one hour? Or fifteen minutes? Even better, instead of arbitrarily tying your clean slate to a day or time, why not create a true and meaningful clean slate through your behavior? Take a brisk walk. Do a brief meditation. Have a chat with a friend. Do some breathing exercises. Write down your feelings for a few minutes. Draw a picture. Allow yourself five minutes of a video that makes you laugh, or some music that helps you relax. Each of these helps reset your mind and productivity much better than the vague "tomorrow."

GOALS AND YOUR VALUES

If you find self-sabotage to be a consistent problem, it is worth asking whether your goals are truly aligned with what you genuinely want in life—whether they truly represent your deepest values. Goals that reflect your sense of purpose (or at least run parallel to it, rather than against it) will always feel more in line with who you are and be more fulfilling to meet. They'll come more naturally too.

Fighting Inertia with the Five-Minute Rule

Even the most motivated and goal-achieving among us are occasionally thwarted by procrastination on a task that just feels "blah." Figuring out that car insurance issue. Unpacking from your trip. Answering that overdue email. These tasks just have to be done; you can only adjust them so much. It soon becomes a question not of how to view the task, but of how to move forward.

That's where the five-minute rule—a trick I've seen help dozens of clients over the years—comes in handy. You simply attack the task for five minutes, and *five minutes only*. Stop yourself when the time is up. (*What's the point?* you might be thinking. *That's barely making a dent in the task.*)

But it turns out, it makes a big dent—because the barrier to beginning something is often the highest barrier of all. The beauty of the five-minute rule is that you cut through the intimidation of starting, and give yourself direction. That builds momentum. Even better, when you force yourself to stop because time's up, you'll be more likely to want to come back to the task later. (Ordinarily, we tend to stop a task when we hit a wall—it's become boring, hard, or confusing. So we leave the task feeling negative about it, which makes us procrastinate even more on returning to it.)

You can reuse this rule again and again with the same task, perhaps expanding the time a little with each work session. But this much is key: Do only an amount that is tolerable and concrete, and make sure you hold yourself to stopping when the timer buzzes.

So, what goals do you want to get started on?

Your Environment Matters Immensely— And You Have the Power to Alter It

Let's say you wanted to avoid spending money for a day. Would you:

a) Fill your wallet with cash
b) Spend the day in your favorite stores
c) Fill your wallet with cash and spend the day in your favorite stores
d) None of the above

Of course you'd choose D to have the best chance at not spending. You'd want to minimize your spending ability (the cash), and also the stimuli that trigger you (the tempting merchandise).

To cut down on sugar, don't go hungry into a coworker's cupcake-filled celebration. If you are a newly recovering alcoholic, don't seek a job as a bartender. To try to make a breakup stay broken up, don't meet your ex at a restaurant with purple velvet couches.

We know all this, and yet when we are looking to make more subtle changes in our lives, we go back to the willpower nonsense. We want to believe that willpower is paramount in summoning the strength to overcome any stimulus or temptation. And when we haven't created an environment that helps us succeed, we blame our inner selves instead of fixing the external situations. And this blame makes us feel even more hopeless about our ability to change—which makes us feel even less in control.

Instead, we must pay closer attention to the environments we create.

What habits do you want to change in your life? Think about the situational triggers that contribute to them, and the ways you can change those triggers.

Stimulus-Response Conditioning Becomes Habit over Time

Often our emotional state is the key link between the stimulus and our response. Let's take smoking, or vaping. If you are looking to quit, you must contend with more than just a physiological need for nicotine. Many people focus only on the nicotine, and start a schedule of cutting back on the number of cigarettes, which seems like a good idea overall. But this has a danger. If you just start diminishing the number of your cigarettes, you'll likely be tempted to "save up" the remaining ones for really stressful occasions when you are already the most emotionally reliant upon smoking. (*If I can have only four cigarettes today, I'd better save one for after I meet with the boss.*) And so although you're lessening your number of cigarettes, you're not lessening the connection between the stimulus (a stressful situation) and the response (wanting a cigarette). In fact, you may even be strengthening that connection, since now the only times you smoke are the times when you really, really feel you need it. You haven't made headway on reducing your *psychological* need for a cigarette in times of stress, even if you have slightly reduced your *physiological* need for nicotine.

A better way to cut down on cigarettes is to randomize the times of day you smoke the remaining ones. This breaks the stimulus-response connection much more quickly, since you'll sometimes have to go without a cigarette even when you most want one. That increases your ability to tolerate stress without smoking—thereby helping break the stimulus-response connection that kept you so beholden to your cigarettes.

If the stimulus-response cycle is so powerful, why not be in charge of which stimuli make the difference for you? If you want to adopt a positive habit, start tying it to something that is going to happen anyway. Maybe you do two push-ups every morning when you get out of bed. (Or maybe you feel that would make you a masochist. Different habits for different folks!) Maybe you always do a calming visualization when you brush your teeth each night. Perhaps five minutes before dinner each evening, you do a quick straightening of your living room. By picking and using a stimulus that happens pretty automatically—like getting out of bed, eating dinner, or brushing teeth—you give the newly connected habit some automatic, natural momentum.

Repetition—and Practice— Build Strength

Habits stick because we've found realistic, sustainable ways to keep them going—and this becomes self-perpetuating, since the more we do something, the stronger the habit becomes. How many times have you mindlessly driven back home, or gotten off at your subway stop, not even fully aware you are doing so? It's become fixed within you. It's not innate or evolutionary for you to make that right-hand turn. You've just had a lot of practice.

I'm always hearing pronouncements about exactly how long it supposedly takes to build a habit. I don't buy them—there can't possibly be just one magic number of days for all human beings or all habits. But it is absolutely true that the more you do something, the more automated it becomes: the more the pathways in your brain know what to do without you telling them. So change your environment to reduce the effort and time that it would take to build the habits you want. Then you can start marking off the days more successfully. This is referred to as stimulus control. Store your athletic shoes right by the door to be more ready for a walk. Have a convenient and attractive landing space for your mail right when you walk in, so that you won't just toss it on the kitchen table. Come up with a list of words that are quick, funny substitutes when you don't want to curse. Have washed, cut-up veggies in your fridge ready for snacking. Keep a koosh ball or even a little bin of "slime" to keep your fingers busy instead of chewing your nails. For some habits, you can even remove the effort altogether, like having your bank automatically siphon off savings and retirement cash into a special account every week.

You can also work this in the opposite way: Make unwanted habits harder to engage in. Tie a couple of extra grocery bags around your sweets and soda when you store them. Disable certain apps on your phone so that you have to access those sites by browser. Block the number of your on-again, off-again, controlling ex-partner. Put your alarm farther away from your bed so that you have to get up to keep hitting "snooze."

Don't keep waiting for motivation or willpower. Your environment can work for you much, much sooner.

Building better habits

When you spend time planning for the right goals and the most functional steps to meet them, the payoff is significant.

I **CHALLENGE** the thoughts you have about willpower. The next time habits are on your mind, observe the stories you are telling yourself about them. Look out for negative thoughts that are unreliable narrators (*I can't help myself*, *I'm just so lazy*, or *I won't ever change*) and reframe them ("This takes effort, but I can take small steps each day" or "Because this means something to me, I will change it").

2 **CHOOSE** one change—a small one is just fine—that you've been wanting to make for a while. (Stumped? What about incorporating more mindfulness practices, like the ones in Chapter 2?) Alter your environment to make this change come more naturally: Remove an obstacle to it, reward yourself for it, have a friend join you in it, set phone reminders for it, or tie it to an automatic part of your routine. Or challenge yourself to work on it for just five minutes. Bonus points if you chose an unusual or inconvenient time of the day to do this, pushing through your inertia.

3 **EXAMINE** a goal that is important to you that you're not quite on track with. Can you identify a tweak to it so that you can gain momentum, rather than being trapped by inertia? For example, "Be better about money" becomes better-defined: Save more? Spend less? Keep better track of it? Think about setting a discrete time period and a specific reward. What is a small, concrete step that you can put into practice today to get yourself going?

You Buy Into the Myth of Arrival

HAVE YOU EVER HAD A SENSE that you aren't really "you" yet? That once you get a promotion/organize your life/get fit/ find a partner/figure out that health concern/make a better living, et cetera, et cetera, et cetera—and there are always et ceteras—you will finally come into being, be able to enjoy yourself once and for all, and become the person you were meant to be?

So many of us feel this way.

But what if you—right here, right now, the person reading this in their frayed yoga pants that have never once been worn to do yoga—what if that *is* the real you?

And what if that is absolutely, positively, 100 percent OK?

You may not believe it's true yet, but that's what we'll be working on in this final chapter: the idea that you are valid and worthwhile exactly as you are, already in this moment right now. That this very time of your life has the potential to be just as rich, rewarding, and engaging as some hypothetical moment in a distant future.

That's right. *You are already enough.*

Of course, for some people, this thinking comes naturally. Such people engage in each day as it comes, not postponing fulfillment until some future date when they have deemed themselves "worthwhile" enough for it. They are usually quite capable of letting themselves be fully present in the real moment, not the future hypothetical one.

But for many of us, that is far from the case. And even if we are able to engage mindfully in some moments or value *parts* of ourselves unconditionally, we still tend to live under the shadow of what we believe to be our deficits. We define ourselves by our unmet goals, our imperfections (or supposed imperfections), or the perceived limits of our day-to-day circumstances.

This is because of the myth of arrival, a pervasive but mistaken belief that only once we "arrive" at some future point will we be ready to fully experience joy or fulfillment. But before we see exactly what the myth entails, let's look at some common ways it shows up.

Sarah and the Checklist-Perfect Life

Sarah was twenty-nine and, by all accounts, extremely successful. She had graduated with honors from a well-regarded college, earned a master's degree in an emerging field, and now worked at her dream job. She had even met the love of her life while in graduate school, and they had married the previous year. Neither of them wanted children, but they had already amassed enough savings to take frequent adventure trips, a love of both of theirs, and to have adopted an adorable schnauzer named Sam. They had recently refinanced their condo, a lovely place that Sarah enjoyed decorating and felt like she could live in forever. By everyone's estimation, Sarah should have been quite happy. Her friends often told her that she seemed to have it all together, while they were still trying to figure out what career they wanted to embark upon, or were stuck in graduate school doubting themselves, or struggling on the dating scene. Sarah had already checked all those boxes. She felt she should be in the absolute prime of her life, that this was the moment she had been waiting for as long as she could remember: the moment when she had it all figured out. The moment when she had finally *arrived*.

So why did Sarah feel so empty?

Jay and "Am I Really a Grown-up?"

Jay was forty-eight and often made jokes about how he had yet to grow up. He felt like he was just bumbling through adulthood, despite being married with two children and having a twenty-year career in pharmaceutical sales. He often had the eerie feeling of waiting for his "real" life to begin. Forty-eight sounded so *old* to him, but he felt like he hadn't done anything yet with his life. He loved his wife and children dearly, but he also felt he had failed in some way. Was this *it*? Wasn't he supposed to do great things? He often spent time online browsing luxury vacations. He had spent the past twelve years in a battle with the fifteen pounds he had put on after becoming a dad, but they never stayed off for long. He constantly told his wife that maybe someday he would be promoted high enough that they could get a bigger house, and he compared himself nonstop with his neighbors and coworkers. Perhaps he was just a late bloomer, and things would all fall into place when he hit fifty—yes, he told himself. *That's* when he'd figure things out and find a way to feel content.

But would he ever?

Mariana and the Boredom of Now

Mariana was thirty-three and always daydreaming about how to better herself. She spent so much on beauty products that her friends teased her about it, and she was notorious for starting new plans—cooking plans, exercise plans, and house redecorating plans—without ever finishing them. The stuff stored in her guest room was like an archaeological site of her past lives: the summer she got really into Zumba, the year she thought she was going to get her computer-programming certificate, the three months she became obsessed with essential oils. She was frustrated about never being able to follow through, but she also could admit that nothing excited her more than turning over a new leaf. It made her feel happy, like the world was full of possibility. Maybe, she thought, she could be the person who had people over all the time for creative, legendary parties. Maybe she still had time to become someone who went running for fun. Perhaps with just a little more effort, she could develop a more impressive career.

And yet this excitement never lasted. Deep down, she felt like she was treading water, unhappily waiting for the *real* part to begin. When would that be?

Rachel and the Case of "Me Last"

Underwear. It all started with underwear.

Rachel was a forty-two-year-old stay-at-home mother. While doing back-to-school clothing shopping for her twin boys, she realized that in addition to shorts, pants, shirts, and socks, they could probably use new underwear. She was sticking to a budget—she always did—and wondered about the quality difference between the four-pack and the six-pack at the same price. As she pondered this, something hit her: Her own underwear was probably five years old. She groaned inwardly every time she put it on, as it was so stretched out and faded. And yet it never really occurred to her to buy new pairs for herself. Sure, she made jokes about it occasionally to her husband, how her underwear wasn't exactly the stuff of late-night fantasies. Or she chuckled with fellow moms as they conducted competitively self-deprecating conversations about what "disasters" they were (the person who had slept the least that week usually won). But even as Rachel recognized that her own needs always tended to come last, she never really took a step back and thought about how to counteract this, or even acknowledged that it was a problem. Simple pleasures had begun to automatically be pushed aside as "someday" treats—things she would finally indulge in at a future point in life, a stage she couldn't quite picture. If she was honest with herself, even certain basic needs started to seem like they weren't quite valid. She sometimes felt like she was on an endurance run, a race to deny herself as much as possible so that she could take satisfaction only in giving, giving, giving. What had happened to her?

What Is the Myth of Arrival?

Sarah, Jay, Mariana, and Rachel illustrate four common ways that the myth of arrival gets put into action, on a practical, everyday level, and we will revisit their individual stories at the end of this chapter. Their lives look very different from the outside, because the myth of arrival trap has manifested itself quite differently in each of them. And yet they all have something very crucial in common. They are stuck in a self-perpetuating cycle that tells them that their now is not as meaningful, enjoyable, or worthy as some ambiguous time in the future. They believe they should postpone their true engagement with life, their true soaking up of experiences. Because of the myth of arrival, they feel that they aren't fully realized humans yet.

The myth lies to us, saying that once we arrive at some future point, everything will magically improve. It makes us feel that only at that point will we finally be happy/satisfied/attractive/confident/organized/prompt/well-loved/rich—or any other magical flavor of nonsense.

Of course, future-oriented thinking can be a positive thing, such as when we set goals that truly motivate us and align with our values. But the myth of arrival makes us look toward the future in a manner that takes *away* from our present lives rather than in a positive manner that helps *enhance* our here-and-now.

Since the myth of arrival tries to convince us that things will fall into place only once we "arrive" at a certain point in our future lives, it's saying that things are forever out of place in our present ones. That if we'll only truly be living at that future point, then we must not really be living now, so why should we try? The more you orient yourself exclusively toward fulfillment for Future You, the more you tell yourself that Present You is unworthy of it.

How the Myth Damages Our Futures

The myth of arrival damages us in several ways: First, it's wholly untrue. There is no point in life when we will suddenly "arrive" at a place that is permanently easier, less stressful, or free of unexpected complications. (Complications are the nature of life. They're what we sign up for by living—and oh, how boring things would be without them!) So if we buy in to the myth, we set ourselves up for heartache—because when we get to the point where we are supposed to have arrived, not much will have changed. If our relationships aren't magically any better, our self-esteem hasn't improved spontaneously (and our hair still does that annoying thing in the back), then we've just given ourselves another excuse to be disappointed.

We may ask anew, "What's wrong with us?" setting the stage for another round of dwelling on our perceived deficits.

Now, maybe you're resisting this a bit, saying that for some goals, it's different. That when you truly arrive at a certain point because of a big accomplishment, you would be immune to this disappointment. After a long-awaited achievement, wouldn't you begin giving yourself celebratory pats on the back that would forever protect you against getting down on yourself?

Well . . . nope. Not likely with the myth of arrival. If you are so steadfast in believing that once you achieve something, your life will automatically shift into a new phase that is qualitatively better than before—emotionally, logistically, socially, behaviorally, even financially—then you're going to be blindsided. First, because of a well-documented experience called *hedonic adaptation*. It's a sneaky and somewhat cruel phenomenon that gradually desensitizes us to a novel, joy-inducing stimulus. We stop appreciating good things as much as we did before, because we become used to them. (Ever listened to a kid complain, just four days after Christmas, about how bored they are? Ever bought a backyard fire pit that ended up being used to make exactly one fire?)

Hedonic adaptation prevents us from resting on the pleasure of our achievements, so it prevents our arrival fantasies from ever becoming reality. Of course, to help counteract this, we can change our focus from pleasure to meaning (Chapter 8). But it's a hard reality-check against the myth of arrival.

There's another reason why meeting even the most stupendous and highly anticipated goal doesn't automatically make you happier: because it often makes life *more* complicated, not less. Even healthy, positive goal attainment can increase our stress, not decrease it, as the new stage of life post-goal brings new challenges. Graduating from school brings a newfound need for independence and self-sufficiency—and figuring out how to buy food on your own dime. Getting a promotion typically means more responsibility and more potential blame, and often longer hours. Making more money comes with more decisions about the "best" things to do with it, just as a larger house comes with more maintenance and more headaches. Committing to a partner—even the love of your life—comes with new challenges of compromising and adjusting your daily living to align with someone else. Having children? Well, the research is clear. It can provide immense meaning and fulfillment, but it tends to put a dent in our day-to-day ease and even happiness in the short-term.

With all of these arrivals, we must newly reckon with the reality that our brains are just as stressed (if not more so) than before, and so we likely start coming up with new beliefs about our shortcomings. We'll become tempted to push things off onto a new arrival point, buying into Myth of Arrival 2.0 (or 17.0!). How easy just to tell ourselves that if only we X, Y, or Z, *then* we will finally have peace of mind and be able to relax!

So myth of arrival begets myth of arrival, reproducing itself more quickly than a pile of rabbits. You'll often decide at that first arrival moment that what's "wrong" with you is that you haven't met some *other* goal yet; you haven't arrived at some magical point in the *new* future. This is similar to the concept of "moving goalposts." You make one field goal, but, wait a minute! Now you've got to do better and make yet another one, farther away. The rules have changed. Your boss might do this to you at some point (what they were happy with two months ago is no longer enough), and perhaps that has familiarized you with how downright annoying, stressful, and demoralizing this practice is.

How Did This All Start, Anyway?

So the damage of this trap is clear. Let's understand more about the ways it develops by revisiting the four individuals whose stories started this chapter.

We do this to ourselves all the time with the myth of arrival.

You arrive, and then you postpone fulfillment all over again, tying it to some fresh arrival point. ("That's it," you tell yourself. "Not this promotion, but the next one." "Not just being in a relationship but getting married." "Not just having a baby, but having a child settled into grade school.") The goalpost gets moved. And how easy to fall into the same trap once that next arrival time comes! After all, by then, the habit has stuck. It's become your go-to coping mechanism for when you feel dissatisfied with your current situation.

Remember Sarah? The twenty-nine-year-old dynamo who has met every goal she's ever had and seems to have the picture-perfect life, though she now feels empty inside?

Her particular brand of the myth of arrival is this:

Sarah lives only for her goals.

Sarah has always lived for the next milestone. Once the milestones are all reached, then—by definition—something feels lacking. Sarah's emptiness comes from defining herself not by who she is, but instead by what she achieves or is about to achieve. In Chapter 9, we discussed how having the right kind of goals can inspire us toward a healthy, satisfying life. So it's not the presence of goals that's the problem. It's the way that Sarah *defined* herself by a lifelong succession of goals, submerging her self-concept to the point where she viewed herself as a function of them. She sees herself as an object on the path to the next accomplishment, like a piece on a game board.

How could Sarah *not* feel empty? She's learned to view the present moment not as something to fully experience for its own sake, but as something that's just a stepping-stone on the way to something bigger and better.

I've worked with many such individuals over the years. The paradox can be jarring—the high-achieving, attractive, goal-conquering person who doesn't seem to have any "problems"—but who feels stagnant and nearly paralyzed by a sense of unease or depression. Often, it's because the myth of arrival has convinced them that happiness will occur automatically someday, as long as they play their cards right. They believed they can achieve their way into a satisfying, meaningful life. But when will they ever have "won"? If there are no more goals to work toward, what do they do with themselves? Since they've always viewed themselves as objects on paths *toward* some-place, they've never learned to find value in the path for its own sake. Instead, they place value only on the destination—the life they're trying to get to, forever just out of reach.

These patterns develop in many ways. Often, the Sarahs in life are admired by everyone else and seem to hold the key to happiness—so no one notices that they've slowly begun to define themselves by the trappings of their external lives. Perhaps Sarah's parents always moved the goalpost, tying affection and love to whether she could meet the achievement standard they had set. Perhaps they always praised her only for her perfect accomplishments, rather than for her efforts, or taught her to contort herself to fit a certain mold or fulfill a checklist that would impress everyone else. Or maybe Sarah had disengaged parents or an unstable home life that she couldn't wait to escape, telling herself constantly that someday she would be done with all that, and *that* would be the way she would make it—by achieving her way out of a bad situation to the next better thing.

Sarah could use work on figuring out what her values really are—deeper, truer, and more profound values than the ones that are just checkboxes for her station in life. She is in dire need of learning to experience her life in the present, and could benefit from a mindfulness practice as a way of centering herself in the moment. Most of all, Sarah needs to spend some time and effort exploring how she came to define herself only through a series of goals. She needs to set new goals that are richer and more inspiring than the ones that left her feeling shallow and lost.

Jay—the forty-eight-year-old father who felt like he hadn't really grown up yet—was very different from Sarah. But he suffers from the myth of arrival all the same. What is his particular version?

Jay has learned to never feel like enough—no matter what.

In Jay's case, his satisfaction isn't directly tied to specific goals (besides fanciful ones he'll likely never meet, like the mansion or the luxe vacation). Instead, Jay has internalized the sense that he is a chronically unrealized person, forever unable to measure up to others. Jay is going through the motions without believing that he is truly worthy of living his life. People like this often suffer from imposter syndrome: They believe they aren't really deserving of the positions they've attained at work, for instance, or consider themselves markedly subpar when compared with others at the same stage of life. Jay deals with discomfort through fantasy, by pinning his hopes on some hypothetical future stage that is less a concrete achievement (like Sarah's) but more a pipe dream of a lifestyle. He latches onto riches, a milestone age, or a certain status as attainments that will bring him fully into adulthood, rather than acknowledging the truth that he has already been an adult for decades—and that it is up to him to let himself fully experience it.

There are aspects of this that people probably find endearing. Jay is probably self-deprecating, doesn't seem to take himself too seriously, and dons the "What do I know?" persona for maximum comic effect—which reinforces it further. Jay probably grew up never feeling good enough as is, denying himself permission to have autonomy in life and just *be*. Maybe his parents never granted him that permission either, always making him feel like he wasn't worthy *yet*—perhaps he had older siblings who always got to do cooler, more independent things, and he was forever the "baby." Maybe he lived in the shadow of another, more accomplished family member, or the world of adulthood was forever a mystery to him because his parents were formal, secretive people who didn't connect with him emotionally or show him what a fulfilling, meaningful life could feel like. Or perhaps they were hyper-controlling and never let him decide anything for himself.

Whatever the reasons, now it's time for Jay to figure out how to stop defining himself by conditions he'll never meet. He needs to do the work to reconcile his feelings of insecurity—which everyone goes through—with permission to move forward in life in ways that he chooses. He's in need of a developing sense of purpose that matters to him and is tied to his daily life, not his fantasy one. *This* is what can help him begin to feel like a fully realized adult.

Yet another manifestation can be seen in Mariana—the woman who was always seeking the next new thing to give her some excitement. She was less paralyzed by unmet achievements per se, but instead downright uncomfortable with even the idea of the here and now. Mariana got bored very easily. But if we look closely, we'll see that in truth, her boredom is discomfort with being fully present in the current moment.

Mariana gets restless with the present
moment, and seeks to avoid it.

Mariana becomes itchy and believes that her life is dull (or maybe even painful) as is—that she constantly needs to restart and seek new adventures. It isn't so much that Mariana feels she needs to achieve certain specific things in life, but rather that she thinks life should be achieving something in *her*: sparking constant excitement. This is compounded by her inability to really value anything she has already achieved, or any of the qualities she already possesses. Mariana believes she is always one small tweak away from true happiness. But the tweaks aren't real because they never stick. They give her only the illusion of movement, not true progress. Mariana is sitting still in angst, rather than learning to sit still in a mindful way that lets her truly engage with her actual life as it is. Mariana lives in fantasy futures that never materialize and can never satisfy.

It's likely that Mariana's had this mind-set for a long time. And as with Sarah and Jay, there are attractive qualities to it—Mariana probably appears energetic and always in motion. Her excitement, even when fleeting, can be contagious (and also, sadly, makes her a prime target for her friends' pyramid schemes). This trait has become reinforced throughout her life: Mariana is the person up for anything. As a child, she was probably quick to daydream or scheme, with exhaustive lists of birthday gift ideas that were outdated by the time her parents gave her the presents. Her attention span and focus may be deficient, and an ADD/ADHD evaluation couldn't hurt. But her constant need to escape her current life also reflects an underlying anxiety with the question: What if life isn't always fun? Mariana has never learned how to sit with discomfort—she wants to fix it by moving on to something new. Perhaps her parents taught her always to be on a quest to "fix" herself—whether by modeling that behavior themselves or by enumerating the ways she fell short. Mariana's also probably learned to misinterpret stability and balance for boredom and ennui, to the point where staying in one place, physically or metaphorically, has become unnerving for her. Maybe something upsetting happened to her that she prefers not to think about, and she's worried that if she's bored her mind will go there. Moreover, Mariana probably never learned to see herself as OK as is: Her self-concept is that of a constant self-improvement project.

Mariana may always be an adventure-seeker at heart, and that can be a wonderful thing. The key for her is to do the work to learn how to choose adventures that will truly be meaningful. She needs to stop the cycle of latching on temporarily to shallow ideas that will never truly click because they were never the right fit. She needs real, honest exploration of what she wants in life, and systematic work on being able to tolerate the itch that misleadingly turns her away from the present.

Finally, we have Rachel. She was the forty-two-year-old mother of two young boys who had become used to denying herself what she'd do for others. And if we dig down deeper with Rachel, we'll see that it's not just about underwear. It's everything. A night out to a restaurant of her own choosing, or a couple of hours on the weekend to pursue a hobby. A moment of quiet on a weekday evening, or a long, uninterrupted phone call with her best friend from high school. All of those things, though she'd love them so much, had been pushed aside automatically as "someday" fantasies—abstract ideas she couldn't allow herself to take part in, because right now they didn't feel acceptable. Though she seems different than Sarah, Jay, and Mariana, she's a fellow myth-of-arrival sufferer just the same.

> *Rachel believes that it is never yet the*
> *right time to prioritize her own needs.*

Rachel has learned to drown her own desires so consistently that the message has been reinforced within her for years: She isn't worthy of satisfaction for her own sake. Satisfaction is acceptable only when it is tied to the satisfaction of someone else. She can feel good for meeting her family's needs, but it is selfish to meet her own. (You could say that Rachel views herself as an object in the meeting of other people's needs, just as Sarah viewed herself as an object in meeting her own various goals.) This made Rachel put off her own desires to some distant arrival point—like, for instance, when someday she didn't have to budget for children. And yet, by ignoring her own self so harshly, she all but guarantees that she'll always feel uncomfortable meeting those needs at all, because her habit of "me last" will have long become stuck.

Falling into this trap happens most often to naturally nurturing, generous people and those in caregiving roles. It's particularly common in mothers, who have the added pressures of society's messages that a mother's denial of personal pleasures is something to take pride in. Some people have had these tendencies since childhood, believing that their happiness doesn't matter as much as that of those around them. Children of dysfunctional parents often learn quickly to try to see to everyone else's needs first, to try to create peace—and to never rock the boat by needing anything themselves. If Rachel grew up with a parent who struggled with alcohol abuse, for example, she likely absorbed early on how to keep quiet so as not to annoy Mom or Dad, and to put on a calm smile while sweeping up the broken bottles.

This is the ugly underbelly of being a "good" person. Rachel is probably praised as a wonderful mother and partner, a caring friend and neighbor, a warm individual who would never deliberately cut in front of someone in line or say no to helping with the PTA's silent auction. Our society is desperately in need of Rachels, and I would be the last to argue against prosocial behavior. But Rachel's own well-being matters too—why should it not? If personal needs and "selfish" pleasures are sacrificed over and over, that can create a stressed, resentful Rachel, a person who feels guilty for being frustrated at the ingratitude around her, and who suddenly screams at her children out of nowhere.

Rachel deserves new underwear. And she could use some help carving out oases in her week: times that are hers and hers alone, experiences that she is allowed to have for their own sake, social time with people who bring her joy and with whom she is in a reciprocal relationship—where she is not unilaterally taking care of them. Even better, Rachel could learn to be taken care of herself sometimes, whether with a simple occasional splurge on a massage, or by redefining the division of household labor with her partner.

Of course, every parent who is doing a halfway decent job has to sacrifice some of their needs for the sake of their child. But when the pattern gets so habitual that virtually all need fulfillment is automatically postponed to some future date—the myth of arrival in action—one's present life feels like drudgery. (And for those of you who believe that relief from drudgery shouldn't be a priority for caregivers, it's worth pointing out that the extra pep in their step and the decreased risk of depression and anxiety will end up helping them take better care of others.)

The Antidote to the Myth of Arrival

We've now seen myriad ways that the myth of arrival takes root in our psyches. It gradually infects our mind-sets to postpone our happiness, and gets us to believe something very toxic: that right now, we are not measuring up. That we are not enough.

The antidote starts with simple awareness, with reminding yourself that you are worthy of enjoyment and fulfillment, right now. How couldn't you be? You must acknowledge that there is no "arriving" in life—except for the time you already did on your very first day here, wailing your first wail, opening your eyes to the world for the very beginning of everything. You were worthy of life then, and you are absolutely worthy now. You are already enough, and always were.

Life is here already. It's been here for you for years, decades even. (Unless you are a particularly precocious nine-year-old with the keenest interest in self-help books that I've ever seen. Bravo!) When you tell yourself that certain things will happen in the future and only then will your real life begin, you are giving up the autonomy of choosing to live your life right now in the way you want. You are postponing joy and meaning, both. You are making yourself feel that you are not deserving of the things that you look forward to—that you aren't a good enough person yet.

But you *are.*

Life is constantly in flux, with highs and lows and business left unsettled. That's the gist of this mind-bending journey—it's not a finished portrait. Goals change. Hopes and dreams get adjusted. Fears and relationships and jobs and Netflix algorithms shift with the seasons. And the only way to keep up and be authentic in the process is to truly listen to yourself, and let yourself ride the ride. When you lock into the myth of arrival, you stop listening to yourself and to what you really want. You cut yourself off from the reality of your present experience, and stop thinking, and being, and looking out the window at what's there right this second. You only have one life and one today, and no one else has the opportunity to live this life you have. It is yours alone, and you have full rights to it. So what are you waiting for? You are already enough.

Valuing the present moment, and immersing yourself in it.

Work on considering yourself worthy of the present moment. There is no "arriving" in life; there is only experiencing each day along the way.

1 **PLACE** a sticky note on your bathroom mirror, or create a calendar reminder that says "I am already enough." No conditions. Period.

2 **THINK** about what you would have done differently today, this past week, or past year, if you were going to die tomorrow. Of course you can't totally live your life this way, as pleasure would get in the way of meaning. (I'd probably eat enough chips and guac that I would die one day early.) But you should not regularly be postponing things that feel worthwhile or that you enjoy, making them "rewards" for the future when life should be rewarding in the moment.

3 **DRAW** four shapes, representing today, tomorrow, next month, and next year. What do these shapes say about how you view the relative importance of today versus the future, in terms of potential and possibility? If today's shape doesn't measure up, why is that? What can you do to expand the way you think of today? If today looks bright, that's good. But does it truly reflect your perspective, or are you just trying to achieve your way into being the perfect self-help student? (Hi, Sarah!) If the latter, keep reflecting upon it, trying to make it real, validating it as you go. And turn back to these symbolic drawings in moments when you find yourself selling short the here and now in favor of the hypothetical future.

Putting It All Together

IT'S HERE: WE'VE REACHED THE END of the traps.

And . . . you didn't keep a journal.

It's OK.

Or maybe you did, in which case you've got a leg up. But whether you kept notes or not, it's time to reflect back upon what worked, what didn't, and everything in between. Maybe there were big ideas that struck a chord with you, but you need to continue to work on putting them into practice. Maybe there were little techniques that you tried right away, but you've slacked off on practicing them as life got busy. Perhaps there were concepts that resonated, but you put them aside because you were afraid to truly address them (or because you just really wanted a sandwich).

Take some time to flip back and jog your memory, refamiliar-izing yourself with the traps we covered.

So how did you do?

Of course, there is no Omnipotent Grader to emerge now, red pen in hand, assessing your progress. I'll likely never know how hard you worked (or, conversely, how you were "reading" all along but your mind was totally elsewhere). But you are here in this paragraph, and that is what matters now. Remember, working on yourself is a lifelong opportunity. Are you willing to be kind enough to yourself to embrace where you are in this very moment, and con-gratulate yourself on the gains that you have already made, even if they are super-tiny and you know you have a long way to go?

Remember, allowing yourself this pat on the back is not mutu-ally exclusive with reflecting on the ways you'd still like to work on things. There can always be more practice. And instead of thinking about that as a deficit, think about it as an opportunity. This isn't about filling holes or fixing flaws, but about deepening and expanding. You are not erasing negative thoughts, but rather growing bigger than they are—and working on your ability to experience them in a way that doesn't fundamentally jeopardize how you view yourself or live your life. Every day you put this into practice, you grow the habit, making it easier to do the next day.

Over the four parts of this book, we've delved into very dif-ferent topics, with lots of specifics, various pieces of research, and all kinds of tools, mechanisms, and theories.

But through it all, the underlying story has stayed exactly the same. It is this: You have the capacity to grow deeper, more engaged, and more authentic than you can even imagine. Don't be afraid to get to know yourself, and to look with an open heart and fully opened eyes at what you find.

And when you have hope (and I've seen people who seem to have reasons as good as anyone's to let go of it, but then they have seen what it can do when they allow themselves to hang on to it), it propels you ahead like few other things can.

You are big enough to feel things deeply and fully, and still move forward—in fact, feeling things in an authentic way helps you do so. Your mind is wide enough to take an honest, genuine look at what it's truly thinking, and to decide—without running away—what to let pass and what to embrace. You can grow open enough to let in your pain; you need not hide from it. You can grieve during the storms and gale-force winds *and also* laugh and love and learn, and embrace the beauty that's still there somewhere, remaining present to greet the sun when it eventually comes out. And you can let all of that connect you with meaning. The self that you inhabit—you, and no one else—does not stop growing when it reaches a certain size or number of experiences. It's a lifelong process.

So, yes, I want you to *feel*. And to think and observe and wonder and stay curious.

And I also want you to *do*. And to connect and explore and take risks and experience, and *live*.

And I hope that you'll let yourself understand that these two ideas go together really, really well.

They are complementary parts of the promise of a life—a life that has the capacity to be as big, wide, and deep as you want it to be. A life that you can't predict, a life that will sometimes hurt, a life that will be imperfect and disappointing at times, but also full of light—cracks and all—if you let it.

Now.

Are you ready to close this book, and open yourself up to that life?

ACKNOWLEDGMENTS

THANK YOU TO MY LONGTIME literary agent Linda Konner. I couldn't be more grateful that I get to benefit from her formidable know-how and magic touch. This lady makes things happen! She knew just what to do to get this book into the hands of people who would be as passionate about it as I was.

And the very best of those people was Cara Bedick, whose enthusiasm, wisdom, and energy kept the fire of this book going throughout my writing it, and whose editing made it immeasurably better. (Even if she axed the jokes about boar entrails and anal itching. Actually, that's probably Exhibit A of how she made the book better.) Anyway, I could never adequately convey my appreciation.

Thank you to Chronicle Prism's managing director, Mark Tauber, who believed in this book from the very beginning and chose to give it a spot in the batting order of their opening lineup. And to the Chronicle design team, who produced beautiful cover options . . . and then kept on producing them, as if they were some sort of art wizards. (Actually, they *are* some sort of art wizards.) I am so grateful.

Thank you to marketing and publicity mavens Jenn Jensen and Shelby Meizlik for helping this book connect with audiences far and wide. And to Betty Anne Crawford of Books Crossing Borders, who added new audiences overseas.

Thank you to my clients, near and far, current and long ago, who have taught me so much more than they will ever realize. It is an honor and a privilege—no matter how clichéd that sounds—to be part of your stories, and to let those stories live on in ways that can help others.

Much appreciation to Steven C. Hayes, whose founding of acceptance and commitment therapy created the foundation for many of the tools in this book, and who has been personally kind in his support.

I would be screwed without the friends who cheered me through yet another "Are you nuts?" deadline: Heidi and Dustin Brown, Monica Silvestro, Holly Morris, Laura Gertz, Kris Kenney, Courtney Creek Blenkinsop, Anne Kingery-Schwartz, Linda Gonzalez Ronan and Rob Ronan, Jen Chen Hopkins, Liz Suiter, Yukari Matsuyama, Marni Amsellem, and the entire DCE (you know who you are!).

A heartfelt thank you to Anna Borges, who was like the doula for the Detox Your Thoughts concept when it was first born at *Buzzfeed*. A fabulous person to be in idea labor with—and beyond!

Humongous thanks to my Baggage Check team at *Express,* who are not only top-of-the-line media professionals but also people that I am thrilled to call friends—Adam Sapiro, Zainab Mudallal, and Rachel Jewett. And to Dan Caccavarro, for bringing Baggage Check to life all those years ago. Thanks to its raucous live chat participants and commenters! That community means so much to me.

Thank you dearly to my students in the Pivot Program, who reminded me every day the differences that the science of psychology can make in a life. And to my undergraduate students at Georgetown. Teaching (and learning from!) you is among my biggest professional passions. Big thanks to my longtime teaching assistant Nicole Conrad, now graduated and off to amazing things, but whose presence over the years never ceased to make my life go far more smoothly. And thanks to Jenn Lynch, who helped a staggering number of new people find my work online.

Thank you to Dr. Lily Gutmann, a psychologist who not only knows her stuff inside and out, but who happens to be one of the most superb calming influences I know.

So much appreciation goes to my family—Mom, Dad, Jeff, Greg, David, Judy, Sybil, Luis, and my wonderful array of siblings-in-law and their children. To be surrounded by the humor, support, and love that you guys bring makes me so, so grateful.

The incomparable Buster showed his support by being inches away from the writing of this manuscript whenever he could finagle it, especially when it was storming outside. Thanks, buddy.

And finally, thank you most of all to Andy, my light and true other half in every sense. Words couldn't do you justice! And thank you Vance, Alina, and Ruby, who crack me up, challenge me, and fill my heart, every single day. Loving, learning, and laughing each day with these four incredible humans—wow. Did I ever hit the jackpot!

NOTES

INTRODUCTION

2: *acceptance and commitment therapy*: S. C. Hayes, K. D. Strosahl, and K. G. Wilson. (2012). *Acceptance and Commitment Therapy: The Process and Practice of Mindful Change* (2nd ed.). New York: Guilford Press.

2: *More than 20 percent . . . anxiety disorder*: B. Bandelow and S. Michaelis. (2015). "Epidemiology of anxiety disorders in the 21st century." *Dialogues in Clinical Neuroscience* 17(3), 327–35.

2: *Depression still remains heavily prevalent*: NIMH. NIMH-Major Depression. www.nimh.nih.gov/health/statistics/major-depression .shtml#part_155029.

2: *The World Happiness Report . . . significant recent declines*: J. F. Helliwell, H. Huang, and S. Wang. (2019). "Changing world happiness." *The World Happiness Report*. worldhappiness.report/ed/2019/changing -world-happiness/.

2: *General Social Survey . . . recent declines*: General Social Survey. (2018). NORC at the University of Chicago. gss.norc.org.

3: *depression and anxiety are caused . . . becoming sticky*: B. Murray Law. (2005). "Probing the depression-rumination cycle: Why chewing on problems just makes them harder to swallow." *APA Monitor on Psychology* 36(10): 38.

3: *are now thought to decrease depression and anxiety*: S. Winston. (2014). "Struggling with unwanted intrusive thoughts." Workshop sponsored by the Association for Practicing Psychologists in Prince George's and Montgomery Counties.

6: *Neuroplasticity—as much as it sounds like*: J. Shaffer. (2016). "Neuroplasticity and clinical practice: Building brain power for health." *Frontiers in Psychology*. www.ncbi.nlm.nih.gov/pmc/articles/PMC4960264/.

CHAPTER 1

18: *mechanism is explained by ironic processing theory*: D. M. Wegner, D. J. Schneider, S. R. Carter, and T. L. White. (1987). "Paradoxical effects of thought suppression." *Journal of Personality and Social Psychology* 53(1), 5–13. doi: 10.1037/0022-3514.53.1.5. PMID 3612492.

28: *your brain likely already creates mental pictures as you worry*: C. R. Brewin, J. D. Gregory, M. Lipton, and N. Burgess. (2010). "Intrusive images in psychological disorders: Characteristics, neural mechanisms, and treatment implications." *Psychological Review.*

30: *It's estimated that 2 to 5 percent of people lack a "mind's eye"*: B. Faw. (2009). "Conflicting intuitions may be based on differing abilities: Evidence from mental imaging research." *Journal of Consciousness Studies* 16(4): 45–68.

31: *You can defuse from a visual as well*: R. Harris. (2008). *The Happiness Trap: How to Stop Struggling and Start Living*. Boston, MA: Trumpeter Books.

CHAPTER 2

35: *there is even similar neurotransmitter activity*: E. Kross, M. Berman, W. Mischel, E. Smith, and T. Wager. (2011). "Social rejection shares somatosensory representations with physical pain." *Proceedings of the National Academy of Sciences.*

38: *with intriguing new research . . . depressive episodes*: A. Adler-Neal, N. Emerson, S. Farris, Y. Jung, R. Coghill, and F. Zeidan. (2019). "Brain moderators supporting the relationship between depressive mood and pain." *PAIN* 160(9): 2028–35. doi: 10.1097/j.pain.0000000000001595.

50: *Bringing nature inside . . . agitation*: M. S. Lee, et al. (2015). "Interaction with indoor plants may reduce psychological and physiological stress by suppressing autonomic nervous system activity in young adults: A randomized crossover study." *Journal of Physiological Anthropology* 34(1). doi:10.1186/s40101-015-0060-8.

50: *The research is as varied*: J. C. Scott, S. T. Slomiak, J. D. Jones, A. F. G. Rosen, T. M. Moore, &and R. C. Gur. 2018. "Association of cannabis with cognitive functioning in adolescents and young adults: A systematic review and meta-analysis." *JAMA Psychiatry* 75(6), 585–95. doi:10.1001/jamapsychiatry.2018.0335.

52: *Mediterranean diet . . . fighting depression*: N. Parletta, D. Zarnowiecki, J. Cho, A. Wilson, S. Bogomolova, A. Villani, et al. 2017. "A Mediterranean-style dietary intervention supplemented with fish oil improves diet quality and mental health in people with depression: A randomized controlled trial." *Nutritional Neuroscience*. doi.org/10.108 0/1028415X.2017.1411320.

CHAPTER 3

76: *clutter . . . higher stress response*: D. Saxbe and R. Repetti. (2009). "No place like home: Home tours correlate with daily patterns of mood and cortisol." *Personality and Social Psychology Bulletin* 36(1): 71–81. doi.org/10.1177/0146167209352864.

CHAPTER 4

88: *Another blind spot . . . negativity bias*: P. Rozin and E. Royzman. (2001). "Negativity bias, negativity dominance, and contagion." *Personality and Social Psychology* 5(4): 296–320.

89: *Confirmation bias . . . problematic*: R. Nickerson. (1998). "Confirmation bias: A ubiquitous phenomenon in many guises." *Review of General Psychology* 2(2): 175–220.

92: *it looms large as another way*: L. A. Festinger. (1957). *Theory of Cognitive Dissonance*. Stanford, CA: Stanford University Press.

99: *research by Martin Seligman*: C. Peterson, S. Maier, and M. Seligman. (1993). *Learned Helplessness: A Theory for the Age of Personal Control*. New York: Oxford University Press.

M. E. P. Seligman. (2006). *Learned optimism: How to Change Your Mind and Your Life*. New York: Vintage Books.

99: *building on the work of Aaron Beck*: A. T. Beck. (1972). *Depression: Causes and Treatment*. Philadelphia, PA: University of Pennsylvania Press.

100: *Originally theorized by Sigmund Freud*: Freud, A. *The Ego and the Mechanisms of Defence.* (1937). London: L. and Virginia Woolf at the Hogarth Press and the Institute of Psycho-analysis.

CHAPTER 5

111: *new research shows that people who are able to label*: D. Y. Liu, K. E. Gilbert, R. J. Thompson. (June 2019). "Emotion differentiation moderates the effects of rumination on depression: A longitudinal study." *Emotion.* doi: 10.1037/emo0000627.

114: *Mindfulness interventions increase pain tolerance*: W. A. Mohammed, A. Pappous, and D. Sharma. (May 2018). "Effect of mindfulness based stress reduction (MBSR) in increasing pain tolerance and improving the mental health of injured athletes." *Frontiers in Psychology.* doi: 10.3389/fpsyg.2018.00722.

124: *David Kessler puts the goal*: D. Kessler. (2018). "Finding Meaning: The Sixth Stage of Grief." Workshop sponsored by PESI, Fairfax, VA.

CHAPTER 6

133: *two different conceptualizations of happiness*: R. M. Ryan and E. L. Deci. (2001). "On happiness and human potentials: a review of research on hedonic and eudaimonic well-being." *Annual Review of Psychology* 52: 141–66. doi: 10.1146/annurev.psych.52.1.141. PMID: 11148302.

134: *research on long-term well-being strongly suggests*: S. Schaefer, J. Morozink Boylan, C. van Reekum, R. Lapate, C. Norris, C. Ryff, and R. Davidson. (2013). "Purpose in life predicts better emotional recovery from negative stimuli." *PLoS One* 8(11), e80329. doi: 10.1371/journal.pone.0080329.

140: *"Flow" . . . by Mihaly Csikszentmihalyi*: M. Csikszentmihalyi. (2009). *Flow: The Psychology of Optimal Experience.* New York: HarperCollins.

CHAPTER 7

153: *with that power comes an even greater vulnerability*: L. Scissors, M. Burke, and S. Wengrovitz. (2016). "What's in a Like? Attitudes and behaviors around receiving Likes on Facebook." Association for

Computing Machinery Conference on Computer-Supported Coopera-
tive Work and Social Computing.

155: *Harvard Grant study run by George Vaillant*: G. Vaillant. (2012). *Tri-
umphs of Experience: The Men of the Harvard Grant Study.* Cambridge,
MA: Harvard University Press.

155: *feeling chronically lonely . . . smoking fifteen cigarettes per day*: J. Holt-
Lunstad, T. B. Smith, M. Baker, T. Harris, and D. Stephenson. (2015).
"Loneliness and social isolation as risk factors for mortality." *Perspec-
tives on Psychological Science* 10(2), 227–37.

156: *number of "kinless" people*: K. Hymowitz. (May 2019). "Alone: the decline
of the family has unleashed an epidemic of loneliness." *City Journal.*

159: *Passively scrolling . . . lonelier*: M. Burke and R. Kraut. (2016). "The
relationship between Facebook use and well-being depends on communication type and tie strength." *Journal of Computer-Mediated
Communication* 21(4): 265–81.

159: *But when we actively engage*: R. Kraut and M. Burke. (2015). "Internet
use and psychological well-being: Effects of activity and audience."
Communications of the Association for Computing Machinery 58(12):
94–100.

159–60: *decades of research . . . do the thing*: U. Fesk and D. Chambless.
(1995). "Cognitive behavioral versus exposure only treatment for
social phobia: A meta-analysis." *Behavior Therapy* 26(4): 695–720.
doi.org/10.1016/S0005-7894(05)80040-1.

162: *research even says that small talk helps our mood*: N. Epley and J.
Schroeder. (October 2015). "Mistakenly seeking solitude." *Journal of
Experimental Psychology* 143(5): 1980–99. doi.org/10.1037/a0037323.

168: *the insights of Allison Slater Tate*: A. S. Tate. (2012). "The mom stays
in the picture." allisonslatertate.com/the-mom-stays-in-the -picture/.

CHAPTER 8

171: *Forgiveness is associated with*: E. L. Worthington, et al. (2007).
"Forgiveness, health, and well-being: A review of evidence for emotional versus decisional forgiveness, dispositional forgivingness, and
reduced unforgiveness." *Journal of Behavioral Medicine* 30(4), 291–302.
doi:10.1007/s10865-007-9105-8.

171: *gratitude boosters . . . provide a measurable mood boost*: D. E. Davis, E. Choe, J. Meyers, N. Wade, K. Varjas, A. Gifford, and E. L. Worthington Jr. (2016). "Thankful for the little things: A meta-analysis of gratitude interventions." *Journal of Counseling Psychology* 63(1), 20–31. doi: 10.1037/cou0000107.

177. *This can bring relief*: S. G. Hofmann, et al. (2015). "Loving-kindness meditation to target affect in mood disorders: A proof-of-concept study." *Evidence-Based Complementary and Alternative Medicine.* doi:10.1155/2015/269126.

177: *slow the aging process*: K. D. Le Nguyen, J. Lin, S. B. Algoe, M. M. Brantley, S. L. Kim, J. Brantley, S. Salzberg, and B. L. Fredrickson. (2019). "Loving-kindness meditation slows biological aging in novices: Evidence from a 12-week randomized controlled trial." *Psychoneuroendocrinology* 108: 20–27. doi.org/10.1016/j.psyneuen.2019.05.020.

CHAPTER 9

199: *goal-setting is an area of our life that is rife with self-sabotage*: K. Nowack. (2017). "Facilitating successful behavior change: Beyond goal setting to goal flourishing." *Consulting Psychology Journal: Practice and Research* 69(3): 153–71. doi: 10.1037/cpb0000088.

204: *we are notoriously bad . . . affective forecasting*: D. Gilbert. *Stumbling on Happiness.* (2016). New York: Knopf.

CHAPTER 10

203: *as shown by the research of C. R. (Rick) Snyder*: C. R. Snyder, ed. (2000). *Handbook of Hope: Theory, Measures, and Applications.* San Diego, CA: Academic Press.

214: *This is because of the myth of arrival*: M. J. Mahoney. (2003). *Constructive Psychotherapy: A Practical Guide.* New York: Guilford Press.

220: *well-documented experience called hedonic adaptation*: S. Lyubomirsky. (2007). *The How of Happiness: A Scientific Approach to Getting the Life You Want.* New York: Penguin Press.

221: *Having children?*: T. Hansen. (2012). "Parenthood and happiness: A review of folk theories versus empirical evidence." *Social Indicators Research* 108(1): 29–64.

ABOUT THE AUTHOR

ANDREA BONIOR, PH.D., a licensed clinical psychologist, is the longtime voice behind the *Washington Post*'s "Baggage Check" live chat and mental health advice column, which ran for fifteen years. Her monthlong "Detox Your Thoughts" challenge for *Buzzfeed* went viral, and she writes a popular blog on relationships and emotional health for *Psychology Today*. Dr. Bonior's expertise has been featured on CNN, *Today, Good Morning America*, NPR, and in the *New York Times, USA Today, Glamour,* and *Refinery29*. She is the author of *The Friendship Fix: The Complete Guide to Choosing, Losing, and Keeping Up with Your Friends* and *Psychology: Essential Thinkers, Classic Theories, and How They Inform Your World,* which was a *Publishers Weekly* best-seller. Dr. Bonior maintains a private psychotherapy practice and serves on the faculty of Georgetown University, where she is a multiyear nominee for the Georgetown College Honors Award, recognized for the impact her teaching has had on students' lives. She lives outside of Washington, DC, with her husband, children, and constantly jumping dog.